Responsive
DESIGN
with WordPress

How to make great responsive
themes and plugins

Joe Casabona

Responsive Design with WordPress
Joe Casabona

New Riders
www.newriders.com
To report errors, please send a note to: errata@peachpit.com
New Riders is an imprint of Peachpit, a division of Pearson Education.
Copyright © 2014 by Joseph Casabona

Acquisitions Editor: Michael Nolan
Project Editor: Nancy Peterson
Development Editor: Eric Schumacher-Rasmussen
Copyeditor: Joanne Gosnell
Proofreader: Scout Festa
Technical Reviewer: Stephen N. Mekosh
Production Coordinator: David Van Ness
Compositor: Danielle Foster
Cover Designer: Aren Straiger
Interior Designer: Danielle Foster
Indexer: FireCrystal Communications

ISBN 13: 978-0-321-95741-2
ISBN 10:   0-321-95741-5

9 8 7 6 5 4 3 2 1

Printed and bound in the United States of America

Dedication

To my parents, Louis and Marie, for their continued support. And to Joe and Jean Rizzi, whose advice, kindness, and patience helped me get to where I am today.

Acknowledgments

I'd like to thank the following people, without whom this book wouldn't be in your hands:

- Stephen Mekosh for not only being a fantastic tech editor and a good friend, but also being the first person to show me both CSS and WordPress.

- Michael Nolan for giving me the chance to write this book and welcoming me to Peachpit Press/New Riders.

- Nancy Peterson and Eric Schumacher-Rasmussen for advice and guidance, editing, keeping me on track, and our weekly talks.

- Joanne Gosnell and Scout Festa for copyediting and proofreading, respectively, and for making it seem like I have a good command over grammar and the English language.

- The design team at Peachpit Press for making this book look amazing.

- Jesse Friedman for the wonderful foreword and kind words.

- Jason Coleman, Stephanie Leary, Lisa Sabin-Wilson, and Pippin Williamson for letting me pick their brains on both WordPress and the art of writing a book.

- My family and friends, especially my parents; my brothers Phil, Mike, and Rob; Dave Redding; Rob McManus; Matt Wren; and my wonderful girlfriend, Erin Holman.

I'd also like to make a quick mention of my brother Phil's website, http://phil.casabona.org. He took the headshot used in this book, and I love his work.

Contents

Foreword

By Jesse Friedman

Today WordPress powers 20% of all websites, and we can look forward to it powering 1 in 4 sites launched in 2014. I launched my first WordPress-powered website in 2005, before all the "cool kids" were doing it. I am very proud to be a veteran developer and strategist for a product used by millions of people all over the world.

Since I launched that first site back in 2005, I have written my own book on developing for WordPress, and I have a few more coming out in spring 2014. I have also contributed to other books and written articles for online publications such as *Smashing Magazine* and *net Magazine*, and I teach both in universities and online. I have also spoken at conferences all over the world, including one where I met Joe Casabona.

I was honored when Joe asked me to write the foreword for this book, because I knew it was going to be great. Joe has a real talent for turning complicated solutions into very simple step-by-step directions. WordPress was built to be simple— simple to set up, simple to install, and simple to extend. Still, it can be somewhat challenging to understand for novice designers and developers who are looking to build on basic WordPress functionality.

These challenges prompted me to write my book *Web Designer's Guide to WordPress: Plan, Theme, Build, Launch* in 2012 and is exactly why Joe wrote his book this year. We are both veteran developers who want to help grow the WordPress community. The best way to do that is to help educate the community and share our experiences and knowledge around a product we use every day. Joe has done just that with *Responsive Design with WordPress*. This is a solid book with lots of great examples.

As a professor at two universities in Rhode Island, I know this book will compliment my class curriculum beautifully. The lessons, examples, and even questions at the end of each chapter help you build a great foundation on WordPress and Responsive Web Design. You also will develop a WordPress theme as you follow along with the book, so you'll be reinforcing the skills you're building as you read.

Not to mention you'll be learning two skills at the same time. You'll be learning WordPress and, at the same time, gaining experience specifically in Responsive Web Design. This approach will not only help to strengthen your skills in both areas but will also make you an expert in a very profitable niche.

As I mentioned earlier, WordPress will power 25% of all websites launched in 2014. This means that 1 in 4 new sites will need a developer who knows WordPress. What's more, as of this year more information is being consumed on mobile devices than on traditional computers. If you didn't have strong skills in Responsive Web Design in 2013, you're definitely going to need them in 2014 and beyond.

In my opinion, there is no better way to learn a skill than by doing it yourself. This book is the best way to learn both WordPress and Responsive Web Design at the same time. Great job, Joe!

Introduction

I got my first portable device when I was a freshman in high school. It was the Palm m100 and I loved it dearly. It didn't do much, and, well, at 13 or 14 I didn't have much to use it for. But having a computer in my pocket? Crazy! As a result, it went everywhere with me (and may have gotten taken away once or twice after I used it in class).

Then I moved to the Compaq iPAQ, which ran Windows and had a color screen. Even crazier, I thought. I could run *real* programs on this. I even asked about campus Wi-Fi when I was visiting colleges in the early 2000s, when it was just becoming popular. I thought of all the amazing things I could do with a tiny computer that came with a pen (stylus) and fit in my pocket. Still, I found myself wanting more after a while. This brings me to my first smartphone: the Palm Treo 650 (**Figure 0.1**).

Figure 0.1 Oh, Treo 650. I still miss you sometimes.

I would do everything on this phone—make calls, take photos, sync my Google Account to it. It even had a primitive browser called Blazer. I could visit websites from my phone!

Since then, of course, the mobile landscape has changed. The iPhone brought a full-featured browser to mobile devices, capable of everything from CSS to JavaScript. It didn't solve one problem, though: the problem of the small screen. That's where Responsive Web Design comes in.

Perhaps you've heard of it. It's apparently pretty popular right now. Lots of people—developers, designers, agencies, and users—are asking about it. And why shouldn't they? On top of catering to what is a quickly growing market, it's pretty cool. Responsive Web Design has become one of those things people check for when they visit a site (resizing a webpage is totally the new "check the source for table layouts").

If you're designing a website, you ultimately have no control over how it's viewed; you don't get to decide where it's viewed or what it's viewed on or the connection on which it's viewed. That might sound scary to some, but to me (and I bet to you, too) it's quite the contrary. I love solving that problem. That's not to say it's not a little daunting. I mean, you need to create a website that is easy to use on mobile but that totally "wows" on the desktop. That's what Responsive Web Design is all about.

WordPress is pretty great too. It powers millions of webpages. Hundreds of millions, even. As you read in the Foreword, it will run 1 of every 4 websites launched in 2014. It does a lot for us while allowing us to do a lot. So how does WordPress fit in with Responsive Web Design? Well, as it turns out, it can be really helpful when creating responsive themes; it has a lot of really great built-in features that we, as developers, can leverage to create better responsive sites. And that's just what I'm going to show you how to do.

Who Is This Book for?

I'd like to tell you that this book is for anyone looking to develop WordPress sites, but in order to get into the real heart of why I wrote this book, I need to make a few assumptions about you, dear reader.

First, I assume you have a working knowledge of HTML, CSS, PHP, JavaScript, and MySQL. I also assume you have some familiarity with WordPress—you've installed it, you use it, you've possibly even coded a theme for it. Finally, I assume you've used a server in some capacity; you should at least know the WordPress directory structure and how to use FTP/SFTP.

So this book is for web developers and WordPress developers who want to take advantage of what WordPress has to offer in order to create great responsive websites. In this book, we are going to cover a wide range of topics and techniques for converting website elements to responsive WordPress theme features.

I will provide a bit of a primer, however. In the first chapter, we will take a closer look at Responsive Web Design: what it is, where it came from, and best practices for using it. Then, there will be a brief overview of WordPress theme development; this will go over some of the major parts of the WordPress theme—important files, the Loop, Custom Post Types, plugins, and more. Then, we'll get into the real fun part.

The real meat of the book—making a responsive WordPress theme—is divided into three parts. Chapter 3 will cover prominent responsive techniques and how to integrate them into the WordPress theme. Chapters 4 and 5 will look at specific components of a WordPress website, including navigation, images, comments, widgets, archives, and plugins.

We will wrap up the book by looking at responsive theme frameworks and child themes in Chapter 6, followed by a cookbook-style section full of tutorials for responsive development in Chapter 7.

Why Did I Write This Book?

When I came up with the idea for this book, there were a lot of things floating through my head. Responsive Web Design is always changing; WordPress is always changing. The best practices of a couple of years ago have changed in both fields, and it's important to get that information out.

There is a big movement in the web development community toward "doing responsive responsibly" (a phrase coined by Scott Jehl); this is the idea that responsive isn't just about screen sizes. There is another big movement in the WordPress community to remove functionality from themes (features such as sliders and Custom Post Types that rely on content). I wanted to create a single place that talks about these things, as a lot of web developers are likely working with both responsive design and WordPress.

Coding Conventions

First of all, any code you come across in the book will be presented in one of two ways. It could be inline, like this: `<?php echo "Hello World!"; ?>`, or it could be in its own block, which looks like this:

```php
function hello_world(){
    $s= "Hello World";
    return $s;
}
print hello_world();
```

Either way, you should be able to recognize it pretty quickly. As far as standards, the WordPress Codex lays out quite a few (http://rwdwp.com/16). I will do my best to adhere to these coding standards.

To denote that the code on the page takes place in the middle of a block of code (that is, there was some code skipped between the first line listed and the next), look for an ellipses (. . .).

A couple of things I'd like to point out: I will be using HTML5 markup here, but we won't do anything with the more advanced facets of HTML5, like Web Sockets or Storage APIs.

In most cases, the CSS will use `.classes` instead of `#ids`. This should make for cleaner CSS while eliminating the need for really specific selectors. All of my CSS will be formatted like this:

```css
.class-name{
    color: #FFFFFF;
    background: #000000;
    }
```

Notice the use of dashes (-) instead of camel case or underscores, and the fact that the closing bracket is also indented. This makes it easier to read the CSS, especially when there is a lot.

Conversely, my PHP function names will always use underscores (_) and be pre-fixed with mf_, like this: `mf_get_featured_images()`.

TIP
Look for text like this in the margins for Tips and Notes.

Finally, sometimes the layout limitations of a print publication mean that we have to stretch single lines of code over more than one line. In those cases, you'll see a light gray arrow (→) to indicate that these lines of code should not be broken when you use them. If you've got the digital version of this book, you may find that code breaks unpredictably in the text. In that case, it's important to rely on the downloadable files (www.rwdwp.com) for accuracy.

Other Book Notes

There is a lot of code in the book. Most of the time I will point out where you can find that code. If I don't, all of it is available on the book's website, www.rwdwp.com, as well as on GitHub. You will also find a list of all the short URLs and the sites they point to.

As you code throughout the book, you'll notice that I don't make much mention of testing before Chapter 6; it's important to test on at least a couple of devices, especially if you plan on using these techniques in production-ready sites (and I hope you do).

Finally, I tend to use a lot of acronyms, which are usually defined in context. In case they aren't, here are the most common ones:

◆ RWD: Responsive Web Design

◆ WP: WordPress

◆ RESS: Responsive Design + Server Side Components

◆ The Codex: the WordPress Codex (or documentation of the API)

Chapter **1**

What Is Responsive Web Design?

If we are being honest with each other, you're probably not here to learn about Responsive Web Design (RWD). You know what it is, and you know the justification. The web is always changing; as of this writing, there are more than 6000 screen resolutions on Android devices alone, and our websites need to adapt! There have been countless books written on the topic since the idea emerged in 2009.

You may have read one of those books or blog posts on the topic from countless authors, or perhaps even implemented your own responsive design already. You're here to learn how to leverage WordPress to improve your responsive designs.

By that same token, we can't just start in the middle. You'll need to learn at least some background before we really dig into it. Trust me, I'm doing this for both of us.

This chapter dives into the history of Responsive Web Design starting with the blog post that launched it all, and then moves into best practices. You'll see the best ways to handle determining and creating breakpoints, other considerations for RWD, and the current state of devices (spoiler alert: There's a lot of device diversity). Because of this, you should at least be familiar with HTML and CSS and the theory behind fluid grids.

Responsive Web Design Origins

Ethan Marcotte coined the term *Responsive Web Design* in his article of the same name for the webzine *A List Apart* (http://rwdwp.com/1). In the article, he says:

Rather than tailoring disconnected designs to each of an ever-increasing number of web devices, we can treat them as facets of the same experience. We can design for an optimal viewing experience, but embed standards-based technologies into our designs to make them not only more flexible, but more adaptive to the media that renders them. In short, we need to practice responsive web design.

The rest, as they say, is history. Mobile is an integral part of society, and people are doing more and more on their phones...but more on that later. Right now, we will talk about implementing RWD and perhaps the most crucial part of a responsive design: the breakpoints.

Breakpoints & Media Queries

Breakpoints and media queries are how we (through CSS) tell the browser when to adjust our designs due to screen size. The media queries themselves aren't necessarily very new; they've been around for quite some time and are supported by most browsers (**Figure 1.1**). Developers use media queries to apply CSS based on specific conditions (e.g., only screens or print, or by browser width). Breakpoints are the browser widths determined by the developer; they are the point at which the layout will change. For example, 1024px can be considered a breakpoint.

CSS3 Media Queries - Recommendation

Method of applying styles based on media information. Includes things like page and device dimensions

Resources: WebPlatform Docs   IE demo page with information   Media Queries tutorial   Polyfill for IE

Global user stats*:	
Support:	87.09%
Partial support:	0.01%
Total:	87.1%

	IE	Firefox	Chrome	Safari	Opera	iOS Safari	Opera Mini	Android Browser	Blackberry Browser	Opera Mobile	Chrome for Android	Firefox for Android
23 versions back			4.0									
22 versions back			5.0									
21 versions back		2.0	6.0									
20 versions back		3.0	7.0									
19 versions back		3.5	8.0									
18 versions back		3.6	9.0									
17 versions back		4.0	10.0									
16 versions back		5.0	11.0									
15 versions back		6.0	12.0									
14 versions back		7.0	13.0									
13 versions back		8.0	14.0									
12 versions back		9.0	15.0									
11 versions back		10.0	16.0									
10 versions back		11.0	17.0		9.0							
9 versions back		12.0	18.0		9.5-9.6							
8 versions back		13.0	19.0		10.0-10.1							
7 versions back		14.0	20.0		10.5							
6 versions back		15.0	21.0		10.6			2.1		10.0		
5 versions back	5.5	16.0	22.0	3.1	11.0			2.2		11.0		
4 versions back	6.0	17.0	23.0	3.2	11.1	3.2		2.3		11.1		
3 versions back	7.0	18.0	24.0	4.0	11.5	4.0-4.1		3.0		11.5		
2 versions back	8.0	19.0	25.0	5.0	11.6	4.2-4.3		4.0		12.0		
Previous version	9.0	20.0	26.0	5.1	12.0	5.0-5.1		4.1	7.0	12.1		
Current	10.0	21.0	27.0	6.0	12.1	6.0-6.1	5.0-7.0	4.2	10.0	14.0	25.0	19.0
Near future	11.0	22.0	28.0	7.0	15.0	7.0						
Farther future		23.0	29.0									

Note: Incomplete support by older webkit browsers refers to only acknowledging different media rules on page reload

Figure 1.1
Browser Support for Media Queries, from caniuse.com

NOTE
When RWD first appeared, "common" breakpoints emerged and were pretty congruent with Apple products, hovering around 320px, 768px, and 1024px.

The advent of mobile devices has spurred the need for media queries and breakpoints. Furthermore, we need to keep in mind that this is still an evolving technology. When Marcotte first introduced Responsive Web Design, there weren't too many popular devices, so some "common" breakpoints emerged.

Since then, the number of screen sizes has grown exponentially in both directions, and different approaches to breakpoints have been proposed regarding both how the breakpoints are represented and how they are determined. What I'm about to outline are not only considered best practices (at the time of this writing), they're also the techniques I'll be discussing throughout the rest of the book.

Em-based Breakpoints

NOTE
Fun fact: Em isn't actually an acronym or short for a word, as px is for pixel. It's a unit of measurement associated with type size and is based on the capital M for the type being used; "em" is the phonetic spelling of "M." In CSS, em has moved away from being associated with a relative type size and is now relative based on browser and container sizes.

In the previous section, you saw the emergence of "common breakpoints" based on the specific pixel widths of browsers. As early as 2011, developers were noticing that these common breakpoints couldn't be relied upon to establish RWD best practice for two reasons. The first has to do with websites adapting not only to the device but also to the user's settings. In her article "The 'Trouble' with Android" (http://rwdwp.com/2), Stephanie Rieger talks about how it's impractical not only to design for specific screen sizes, but also to presume we know what the user's device settings will be. While the browser assumes some defaults for font sizes, margins, and more, users have the ability to change the defaults to better suit their needs. If a user has trouble reading small text, for example, he or she could increase the default size of text. As long as a website is coded properly, the font size will automatically increase with the user's settings. For this reason, we should move from pixel-based breakpoints to em-based ones.

Web developers have actually been using ems to define element sizes for years. This is because the key to flexible text that will not break with browser settings is text with font sizes based on ems, not pixels. This is very important to remember: pixels are absolute values. If font sizes (and other elements, for that matter) are defined using pixels, they will not change regardless of the user's preferences.

By using ems for font size, our font is sized properly based on our design as well as the user's preferences, so if the user zooms his or her browser, our design does not break. This same technique can be applied to breakpoints, where instead of using pixels, we use ems to define where our design changes. This ensures that the website's layout is flexible and responsive, not only to the width of the browser but also to the user's settings. In other words, it puts the user in complete control of how he or she views the content.

Converting Px to Em and Percentages

Determining px to em is pretty simple: Em represents 16px, so 1em = 16px. Of course, there are also a lot of resources to help you convert. My favorite is www.pxtoem.com. It will do the conversions both ways, as well as change the base pixel value for you.

Of course, as you drill down (or cascade down, if you will), it won't be so simple, as elements inherit their styles from the parent elements. This means if the font size is 20px, your base value is 20px, not 16px. But don't fret! Ethan Marcotte offers a simple mathematical solution for figuring out your em value:

```
target/content = result.
```

So if your base font size is 20px and you want your font size to be 24px, you would calculate 24/20 = 1.2, so your font size would be 1.2em. Similarly, if you want it to be 16px, you would calculate 16/20 = 0.8, or 0.8em.

With layouts, you can do the same with percentages. So if you decide you want your layout to be based on a 960px grid, your content would be 960px. If you want the main content area to be 600px, you would get the flexible (percentage) width by calculating 600/960 = 0.62. Multiply by 100 to get 62%.

This falls perfectly in line with what RWD is all about: we don't know what devices users will view our sites on, therefore we should design in such a way that they will look good on any device.

So it makes sense that flexible, em-based breakpoints are the way to go to ensure the greatest amount of flexibility in a layout. However, there is one more thing we need to do with regard to media queries in order to make them as device-agnostic as possible.

Content-based Breakpoints

Going back to the notion of "common" breakpoints, developers would essentially build for three (or so) devices; namely, the desktop, the iPad, and the iPhone. So instead of locking your design to one device, you're now locking it to three devices. That's an improvement, but a very minor one given the hundreds of devices now available to consumers. With the constant stream of emerging devices and the quickly diversifying pool of screen resolutions, it's a near-impossible task to determine which screens you should design for. That's why what has now emerged as best practice is determining breakpoints based not on device, but on content. Rieger lays out the reasoning for this sort of development in her article.

TIP
For breakpoint checking, I use a Chrome extension called Window Resizer, available at http://rwdwp.com/3

By determining breakpoints based on content, we are finding where our design breaks and fixing it there instead of figuring out the devices on which we want our design to look good. In the screenshot in **Figure 1.2,** my logo/avatar starts to eat the page, so I need to add a breakpoint there to properly size the image.

Figures 1.3 and **1.4** show another of my websites where the buttons only extend to 50% of the screen at a certain point, completely breaking the design. This is where a breakpoint should go.

In both instances, I need to check to see what the website looks like as I widen the browser window, and then mark down the em value at the point where the website's design changes or looks bad.

Figure 1.2 My website as the browser window expands

Figure 1.3 A small side project of mine in the mobile view

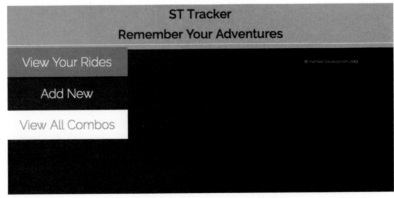

Figure 1.4 The same project expanded out to about double the width

The Current State of Devices

In the last two sections, you looked at how to represent breakpoints in the most flexible way possible. Now it's time to look at why it's crucial to determine break-points on content rather than devices. There are over 6,000 screen resolutions on Android alone—something I first heard from Luke Wroblewski in a talk from 2012. A cursory search for "most popular mobile devices" brings up scores of blog posts, articles, and stats outlining the top 10, 20, even 50 mobile devices. Brighthand.com, a smartphone news blog, publishes the 41 top devices according to their last 5 days of traffic. If we look at my collection of devices, most of which connect to the Internet, we have:

Table 1.1

DEVICE	SCREEN SIZE*	RESOLUTION*
Samsung Galaxy SIV smartphone	5 inches	1920x1080
Google's Nexus 7 tablet	7.02 inches	1920x1200
Apple's iPhone 4S smartphone	3.5 inches	640x960
Apple's new iPad tablet (3rd generation)	9.7 inches	2048x1536
Sony's Google TV box (1st generation)*	55 inches	1920x1080
Microsoft Xbox 360*	55 inches	1920x1080
Sony PlayStation 3*	55 inches	1920x1080
Google Project Glass Prism Projector**		640x360
Amazon Kindle Ereader	6 inches	600x800

*For devices that connect to TVs, I used my TV's information.

** Equivalent of a 25-inch HD screen from 8 feet away

That's a lot of devices, and I'm just one guy! If I visit my family's home, we'd have to add the iPhone 5, the HTC 8.X running Windows Phone, a Kindle Fire (2nd generation), and several other devices my parents and brothers own. StatCounter Global Stats has a graph of the 14 most popular mobile screen resolutions (**Figure 1.5**).

Figure 1.5
StatCounter's Top 14 mobile screen resolutions from May 2012 to May 2013. Notice that more than 40% are in the "Other" category. [Source: http://rwdwp.com/4]

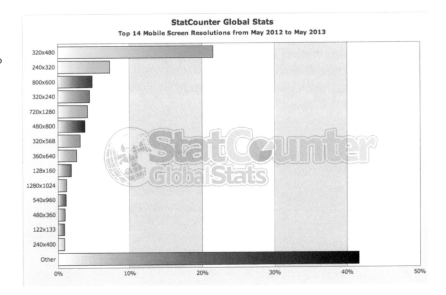

It would be impractical to try to design for all of these devices or screen resolutions, and impossible to predict what the graph would look like a year from now. That is the biggest reason why determining breakpoints based on content and not devices is incredibly important for a good user experience.

Consider Connection Speeds

This is not a comprehensive book about RWD in general, nor is it an overview of mobile development, but in wrapping up this section I want to mention some final aspects of RWD that are important to create a good user experience. After all, a great design or great content will be lost on the user if the overall experience is not good.

Use Discretion!

If you're smart about using JavaScript libraries, CSS frameworks, or other extra code, the experience for users won't be bad. There are a few libraries I use that add value to the website without bogging it down too much. Some questions to ask yourself:

1. Why do I have this library?
2. Is there a better way to accomplish my goal?
3. Do I need everything the library has, or can I trim it down?
4. Some goals I accomplish with JavaScript libraries and snippets:
   - HTML5 support for IE
   - Media Query support for IE
   - Mobile navigation display (on occasion)

Remember: Not everyone is going to be on the fastest Wi-Fi or 4G when viewing your site. Users might be on 3G, weak Wi-Fi, or even Edge. Keep your websites as lean as possible. This means don't load superfluous JavaScript libraries or massive images if you don't need to. This is incredibly important because, as Brad Frost points out, 74% of all users will abandon a site if it takes more than 5 seconds to load. While things like jQuery can be helpful, if they are big and don't add a lot of value, they aren't worth exploring.

Website performance goes beyond this, however. I've seen a lot of sites implement CSS that will hide certain sections of a page, depending on the breakpoint, in order to reveal more "screen-optimized" sections. While the intention is good, the result may be bad because you're forcing the user to download extra markup/code.

NOTE
Remember: CSS can weigh a lot. Optimize your style sheets, and combine them when you can.

If someone is using a smartphone, they will never see the HTML for the desktop, even though they just downloaded it to their device. Things like this can add up, especially if you're hiding images or other multimedia. This, for me at least, is the most compelling reason to consider a "Mobile First" approach to designing websites.

Mobile First!

In Luke Wroblewski's book *Mobile First,* he talks about building websites from the smallest screen out. He argues (and I would agree) that it forces you to consider the most important features and UI elements, as you're designing for a small screen. This will also affect what kind of libraries and effects you use.

When I approach a design "Mobile First," I'm less likely to include extra images and features that ultimately will take up space. As I expand out, I carry these thoughts with me.

There are other file optimizations you can make to lighten your user's load. Regarding images specifically, and thinking ahead to of some of the techniques we'll look at in later chapters, you can run your images through tools that will decrease the file size without removing quality. On a Mac, you can get ImageOptim (http://rwdwp.com/5) . On the PC, there is RIOT (http://rwdwp. com/6). (**Figure 1.6**)

Figure 1.6 An image optimized with ImageOptim. The original is on the left, and the optimized version is on the right (size reduced by 10%). Photo by Philip J. Casabona

Finally, as we look at some tools, particularly JavaScript, you will see a size, "after minified and gzipped." Minifying a file means removing extra spaces, lines, and comments from a file to reduce the size. Another way you can do that is having your server Gzip the files before sending them to the user.

This is something you will have to set up on your server. Through a few settings you can tell your server to serve up certain files compressed by default. In general, HTML, CSS, and JavaScript should be gzipped. Files like images are already compressed.

TIP
For more information on how to use gzip, there is a great tutorial at http://rwdwp.com/7

Curious about your connection speed? Figuring it out is pretty easy. Just follow these steps!

1. Open your favorite browser, and head to www.speedtest.net
   or
   on your mobile device, download the Speedtest app.

2. Click the Begin Test button

3. Watch as it:

   ◆ Pings a server from your machine

   ◆ Gets the download speed

   ◆ Gets the upload speed

When it comes to websites, you should be interested in the download speeds. At home, you can get around 30mbps (I actually get 70mbps at work). 4G will be around 5mbps, maybe 9 on a good day. 3G, however, can be really low—1mbps, even less. That's when page weight can really affect the user.

We will really take advantage of WordPress for this sort of thing.

Wrapping Up

That successfully concludes my primer on Responsive Web Design. I hope you found it helpful, because now we are going to get into the real reason you're here. Together, we are going to answer the question "How can I use WordPress to make great responsive sites?"

From here on out, we'll look at techniques and implementations in WordPress themes for best RWD practice using built-in WordPress functions, lightweight JavaScript, and server-side detection. The last part of the book will be "cookbook" style tutorials for responsive UIs in WordPress.

Questions

1. Who coined the term "Responsive Web Design"?

2. Why is it important to use em-based breakpoints over px-based ones?

3. What is the best way to determine breakpoints?

4. What are some other things you need to consider (besides screen size) when creating a responsive website?

Answers

1. Ethan Marcotte coined the term in his article of the same title in *A List Apart*.

2. Em-based breakpoints are more flexible than px-based ones and adjust with the user's personal settings.

3. The best way to determine breakpoints is based on the content: selecting a breakpoint when the content starts to look bad.

4. In addition to screen size, you need to consider connection speed, page size, and the most efficient way to accomplish your goals without burdening the user.

Chapter 2

Creating a Basic WordPress Theme

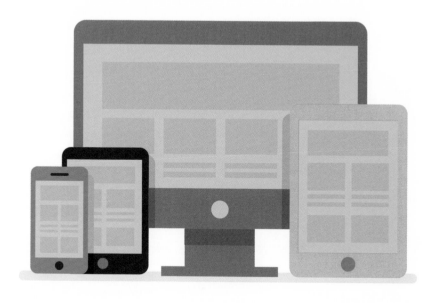

WordPress did something pretty ingenious with their platform. They completely separated content from function from design. Smartly, WordPress' themes and plugins let you manage content, look and feel, and features completely independently of one another. This separation of concerns is something you should keep in mind when developing for WordPress; it's something that will be covered quite a bit in this chapter. As a matter of fact, in this chapter, you will dive right into coding within WordPress, and it's important that you remember this separation.

There are tons of files in the WordPress directory, organized nicely and named intuitively. Everything you need to worry about will be in /wp-content/. This is where both the /plugins/ directory and /themes/ directory are kept (**Figure 2.1**).

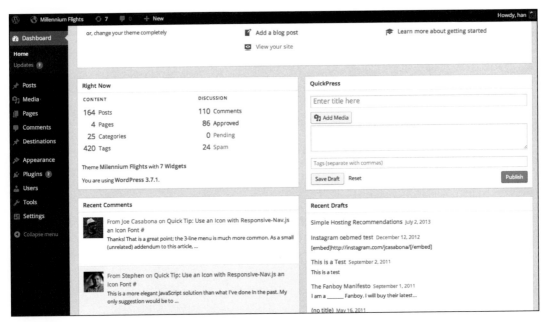

Figure 2.1 The WordPress Dashboard shows you recent site activity and stats right when you log in.

Moving forward, you are going to spend most of your time in the /themes/ directory working on look and feel, but some of the topics we talk about will fall more under the category of functionality or content, which work better when placed into plugins. You don't want to tie content or functionality to the design of your

The WordPress Codex

Moving forward, the WordPress Codex (or just "The Codex") is going to be an indispensable resource. It's the most extensive documentation on WordPress and the number-one site for learning about WordPress APIs. It also has lots of sample code, change logs, and best practices. In short, it's your best friend as you develop WordPress themes and plugins.

Visit The Codex at http://rwdwp.com/8.

site. An important rule of thumb to consider when trying to determine if something belongs in a theme or a plugin is asking yourself, "Would I want to keep this if I redesign the site?" If the answer is (or could ever be) "No," make it a plugin. If it's "Yes," consider if what you're adding applies strictly to look and feel. If it does, it probably belongs in your theme.

"Would I want to keep this if I redesign the site?"

There has been a trend toward feature-loading some commercial WordPress themes so users feel like they are getting more value. But there's a massive drawback to this. If you feature-load themes with things that don't directly affect the design of the site, then site owners and users will lose those features if they do a redesign. Custom Post Types (CPTs), which allow you to add different forms of content to WordPress sites, offer a good example of the potential problems. Let's say, for example, you have a business CPT built into your theme, which you then use to build a business directory. If you change out or disable that theme, you'll *lose all of that content*. You'd have to copy the CPT out of the theme and into the new one, which may not be an option for some users; if a user doesn't have direct access to the server, he or she cannot change the theme on the code level. The same goes for features like image sliders, payment gateways, or anything else that doesn't strictly pertain to design.

With that caveat in mind, it's time to take a close look at theme development. We will cover four topics: Template Structure, The Loop, Custom Post Types, and Plugins.

NOTE

Modifying anything that is not in /wp-content/ is known as modifying the Core, and is a mortal sin in WordPress development. By modifying the Core, you are placing changes in files that will be overwritten during the next update (which some hosts do automatically). All changes made will be lost.

Meet Our Website

Now is as good a time as any to introduce the site we will be working on for the rest of the book. It's a website for a space travel agency called Millennium Flights. Throughout the book, we will be taking our HTML/CSS design and converting it to a fully responsive WordPress theme (**Figure 2.2**). How fun!

Figure 2.2 Meet Millennium Flights, our soon-to-be WordPress theme.

Template Structure

As you develop a *theme*, which is the blanket name for the entire design of a WordPress site, you create individual templates that control displaying certain aspects of the site, such as posts, pages, CPTs, and so on. Under WordPress' hood is a very sophisticated template hierarchy that displays content based on how the theme files are named. The only pages that are actually required to make a theme work properly are style.css and index.php, which is the template that

WordPress uses if there are no other templates available in the theme. That said, you can design a multitude of different templates for pages, single posts, category pages, tags, taxonomies, and more. For even more control, you can get specific with pages, tags, categories, and post types. For example, if you had a CPT named "businesses," you could create a template named single-businesses.php, which would automatically be used to display posts of that type. In the event that you had that CPT but no specific template for it, WordPress would fall back to a different template, single.php, or if single.php doesn't exist, index.php. You can see the entire fallback structure in **Figure 2.3**, The WordPress Template Hierarchy.

While we won't look at every aspect of this hierarchy, let's cover the basics before we move onto the fun stuff—actually building the responsive theme!

TIP

Jesse Friedman's *The Web Designer's Guide to WordPress* does a fantastic job of covering many aspects of Word-Press not explicitly covered here.

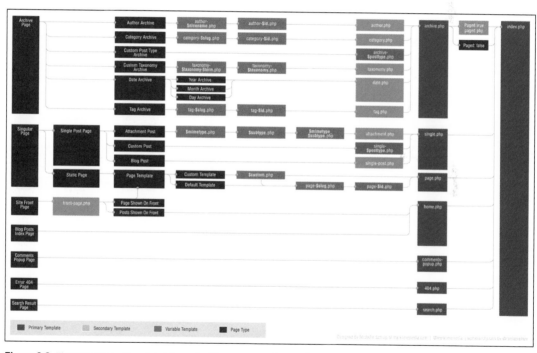

Figure 2.3 The WordPress Template Hierarchy. You can see an interactive version of this flowchart at http://rwdwp.com/9.

style.css

It makes sense to start with the style.css file for the simple reason that this is where your theme is defined. Aside from the site-specific CSS that goes in here, every style.css file starts with something similar to this block of code:

```
/*
Theme Name: Millennium Flights
Theme URI: http://www.millenniumflights.com
Description: A custom theme for Millennium Flights, Inc.
Version: 1.0
Author: Joe Casabona
Author URI: http://www.casabona.org
Tags: blue, white, two-column, flexible-width

License: GPL
License URI: http://www.gnu.org/licenses/gpl.html

General Comments can go here, but are optional.
*/
```

NOTE

The words listed on the "Tags" line are used by WordPress to make your theme searchable based on those keywords, known as tags. The list of all allowed tags can be found at http://rwdwp.com/10.

This block tells WordPress everything it needs to know in order to list a theme in the Themes > Appearance section of the WordPress admin. The only thing found on the admin panel that is not mentioned in this comment block is the associated screenshot. That is a separate file called either screenshot.png or screenshot.jpg.

Regarding the CSS for the site, the WordPress Codex makes some recommendations based on general best practices, such as "use valid CSS when possible," "cut down on browser-specific hacks," and "include a print.css file." In addition to these recommendations, I also recommend that you consolidate all of your CSS into *one* file.

It's common practice for developers to separate the CSS into four different files (names may vary): reset.css, master.css, fixes.css, and style.css, which would just call the other three. As mentioned in Chapter 1, responsive web design is about more than just making a website that resizes; it's about creating a good experience across all platforms. If a user has a limited or slow Internet connection, more requests means slower performance. Instead of using four style sheets, you can use one and remove three requests to the server that eat up bandwidth the user may or may not have.

Another Codex recommendation worth noting is a set of some common CSS styles used for aligning images and styling captions, which is helpful if that wasn't at the forefront of your mind in the design stage. You can find that at http://rwdwp.com/11. Perhaps even more helpful is wpbeginner's complete list of WordPress-generated CSS classes, which you can find at http://rwdwp.com/12.

functions.php

Even though I said WordPress themes only need two files—style.css and index.php—I want to save index.php for last. The next three files we'll look at are going to be instrumental in building a proper index.php, so we'll get those out of the way first, starting with functions.php.

The functions.php file is a place for your miscellaneous PHP code. You can use it to add features like sidebars, navigation menus, thumbnail support, your own php functions, theme options, and more. As a matter of fact, The Codex describes it as a "plugin" file for your theme. It may not be necessary, but it's very helpful. I generally use mine to define constants I use throughout the theme as well as some common functions I found myself using over the years. It's good to keep things organized and not just dump anything and everything in this file, but it can serve as a central place for added functionality.

In this book, functions.php will also be used to do things like server-side detection of screen resolution so you can serve up different templates based on the device the user is using.

A couple of things to note about the functions.php file:

◆ You can use WordPress Hooks to tap deep into WordPress. You can do things like modify the RSS widget, add a custom logo to the login screen, change the excerpt length, or even modify the output of the `the_content()` function.

◆ You can define your own functions, which will all be applied site wide, including in the admin panel. Remember to prefix any functions or classes you write to avoid conflicts. You should do the same thing with plugins and short codes as well.

◆ When working in functions.php, try to be aware of what you're adding; remember to ask yourself if you'd want to keep what you're adding in a redesign. Things can get a bit blurred when working in this particular file.

TIP
You can even use a media query for print instead of using a separate print.css file. All you'd have to do is add the following bit of code somewhere in your CSS: `@media print{ // CSS goes here }`

NOTE
If you read my previous book, *Building Word-Press Themes from Scratch*, you might recall I suggested that functions.php would be a good place for your CPTs as well; however, as I mentioned at the beginning of the book, better practices tell us to make them their own plugin.

header.php and footer.php

The header.php and footer.php files will most likely be the template files you call the most frequently in your theme because they contain just about everything that's not part of the body content. Regarding header.php, anything above the content area will probably go in this file. This includes the HTML, head, and beginning body tags, as well as possibly the site name, search bar, and navigation. You use the function `get_header()` to call the header in a template file. Similarly, with footer.php, the file includes anything below the content area. This will close out the body and HTML tags, and will most likely include the site footer, Google Analytics, and anything else that might belong at the bottom of the page, before you add the `</body>` and `</html>` tags. For this, you use the function `get_footer()`.

NOTE

The only requirement for both `wp_head()` and `wp_footer()` is that they need to be loaded in the page's `<head>` and `<body>`, respectively, to work properly. If you want to make a stand-alone page without using the theme's layout, for example, you wouldn't explicitly need to place `wp_head()` in header.php and `wp_footer()` in footer.php, as long as they are placed correctly.

Also most often included in the header.php file is a very important WordPress function: `wp_head()`. This function will make sure that the webpage loads any scripts, styles, and information from plugins. For example, if there is a plugin for a jQuery slider that uses `wp_enqueue_script()` to load some JavaScript file (or even if you use `wp_enqueue_script()` in your functions.php file), WordPress will know to load that JavaScript file in the head because of `wp_head()`. If you do not call `wp_head()`, there's a pretty good chance things will break. It should be added right before the `</head>` tag.

The footer.php file is the most likely place for `wp_head()`'s counterpart, `wp_footer()`. This function should be called right before the `</body>` tag and is tasked with loading any scripts, styles, and text that will be added at the bottom of the webpage. Again, if you use `wp_enqueue_script()` and set that parameter `$in_footer` to `true`, the function will try to load the JavaScript file in the footer. Without `wp_footer()`, this would not happen.

Aside from the inclusion of these functions, header.php and footer.php look like pretty standard website headers and footers you'd find on any site. As a matter of fact, here is the footer.php file we are using on the Millennium Flights site:

```
</div>
<footer>
        <aside class="group">
            <?php if ( !function_exists( 'dynamic_sidebar' )
            →|| !dynamic_sidebar('Footer') ) : ?>
            //Footer Widgets Go Here
```

```
<?php endif; /* (!function_exists('dynamic_sidebar') */ ?>
</aside>
        <p>&copy; <a href="http://milleniumflights.com">
        Millennium Flights</a>, <?php print date('Y'); ?>.</p>
    </footer>
</div>
<?php wp_footer(); ?>
    </body>
</html>
```

Now—with all of your ducks in a row regarding style.css, functions.php, header.php, and footer.php—it's time for the main event.

index.php

The index.php file is what makes a WordPress site work. As you can see from Figure 2.3 earlier in the chapter, every template page in a WordPress theme falls back to index.php. This means all posts, pages, CPTs, archives, search results, author pages, and other elements will, by default, use the code in index.php if no other template exists. In essence, as long as your index.php page has the right code, you can display every piece of content you enter in the WordPress admin with it.

In the index.php file, you should find three important sections: a call to the header function, `wp_head()`; a call to the footer function, `wp_footer()`; and the all-important WordPress Loop, which we'll talk about in the next section.

Really, just as on any website, the index.php file's makeup will depend on what you want to have on the site; the big difference here is that it can literally be the makeup of every page on the site. Of course, this generally isn't the case because theme designers include other templates, but it's still something to consider when moving forward.

The most important thing to remember is that if you want a custom home page, *do not* make it the index.php page. If you do that, you will almost definitely break a page such as the search results (search.php) or the archives page (archives.php). Instead, you should create a page template (perhaps called page-home.php) or take my recommended approach and use the WordPress Template Hierarchy. There are two approaches you can take: home.php and front-page.php. As far as hierarchy goes, home.php will take precedence over index.php, but only on the

NOTE
The common practice is to let index.php control the display of the most recent blog posts, and perhaps search results and archives. Everything else is left to other template files.

websites's home page, so if you want The Loop on the home page to be different from every other page, create home.php and WordPress will take care of the rest. However, if you want a "static" home page (i.e., one that isn't just a list of the most recent posts), you should use front-page.php. The way WordPress handles the front-page.php page can be demonstrated by a common use case:

1. Create a front-page.php template in your theme.

2. Create a page in the WordPress admin, say with the title "Home Page."

3. Go to the Settings > Reading page in the WordPress admin, and change "Front Page displays" from "Your latest posts" to "A static page."

4. Choose Home Page from the drop-down menu.

No matter what page template Home Page is using, front-page.php will now take precedence (**Figure 2.4**).

Figure 2.4
The Reading settings in the WordPress admin, where you can choose a static home page

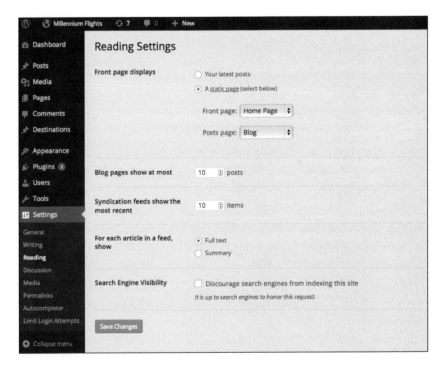

Now we have what I consider the most important files in a WordPress theme, but we still need a way of getting our content out of the admin and onto the website. That way is The WordPress Loop.

The Loop

The WordPress Loop is nothing less than the life force of any WordPress-powered site. It is how all content is displayed on any template, so it's imperative to know how it works. Here's what the WordPress Codex has to say about The Loop (http://rwdwp.com/13):

The Loop is used by WordPress to display each of your posts. Using the Loop, WordPress processes each of the posts to be displayed on the current page and formats them according to how they match specified criteria within the Loop tags. Any HTML or PHP code placed in the Loop will be repeated on each post.

Essentially, WordPress has a set of functions to:

1. Make sure that you have posts to display
2. Display those posts.
3. These particular functions, called Template Tags, allow us to fully customize how you display the information from each post. The content is pulled based on a query that is sent to the page you are accessing; the query is derived from the URL.

While every Loop in a particular template can be different (for example, single.php and page.php can have different Loops), they all have the same basic construct.

Page URLs in WordPress

By default, a WordPress URL will look something like this: http://www.example.com?p=123. In this instance, p is a variable representing a post's ID.

WordPress has an incredibly sophisticated linking structure known as permalinks, which allows you to create pretty-looking URLs with better information, like the publish date, post title, and more. These can be managed from the WordPress admin, in Settings > Permalinks. The Codex has a really in-depth page at http://rwdwp.com/14.

The Construct

The first thing to know is that a template isn't necessarily limited to having only one Loop on it, but there is a Loop that will handle the initial query that's passed to the page. I will refer to this Loop as the "Main Loop" and all other Loops as "Secondary Loops."

The Main Loop in a template starts out like this:

```php
<?php if ( have_posts() ) : while ( have_posts() ) : the_post(); ?>
```

What's going on here? Three WordPress functions are called:

◆ have_posts() makes sure there are posts to display. If there are no posts, have_posts() will return false.

◆ The same function will continually keep track if you still have posts, which is why it's used as the "while" condition.

◆ the_post() unpacks the next post in the queue.

Again, since this is the Main Loop you are working with, your posts are based on the query passed to the page. You could actually overwrite the original query by using WP_Query() or get_posts() to get customized information, but we'll talk about that later. No matter what, as long as that query returns posts, have_posts() returns true and you enter The Loop.

You'll end The Loop in this way:

```php
<?php endwhile; else: ?>  <?php _e(&lsquo;No posts were found.
→Sorry!'); ?>  <?php endif; ?>
```

You have a simple fallback here in the form of an if/else statement: In the case that have_posts() returns false, it tells the user that there are no posts for them. Inside The Loop, you can do all kinds of things to completely customize the post display. All of the template tags can be found in The Codex, and they are pretty intuitively named so you can get an idea of what is available to you. There are tags for the_title(), the_time(), the_content(), the_excerpt(), the_category(), the_tags(), the_permalink(), and much more. It's really worth checking out all tags that are available to you, because you can do quite a bit using them.

All of the tags automatically print the information returned to them, but if you decide you don't want this information printed automatically, most of these functions have accompanying "get" functions—that is, `get_the_title()`—which would simply return the value instead of printing it. Here are a few of the template tags and what you can expect:

◆ `the_content()`: This will display the content of the post, which is whatever is entered into the editor on the admin side. On a single template page (e.g., single.php), the entire content will be printed. On a page where multiple posts are displayed, only the content up to `<!--more-->` will be displayed. If `<!--more-->` is not added in the post's content, the entire post will be displayed.

◆ `the_excerpt()`: This function gets the first 55 words of the post, appending […] to the end of the string. It accepts no arguments. Both the number of words and the ellipsis (…) can be changed within the functions file using filters.

◆ `the_permalink()`: Gets the post's or page's absolute URL in the format defined by the WordPress admin panel in Settings > Permalinks.

Multiple Loops

Aside from the Main Loop, there may be times you want to include a second Loop on your page, perhaps to display other posts, secondary content, images, or something else entirely. Luckily, WordPress has some ways to handle this case.

There are actually several ways to do this, including one that's resoundingly considered "the wrong way." There's a function you may come across in The Codex called `query_posts()` that will, in most cases, modify the posts or display the content you want. However, this is the same function the Main Loop uses, so calling it might cause conflicts with the displayed content. You may end up having two different titles, the wrong content, or other unpredictable issues.

NOTE
Even The Codex page for `query_posts()` says not to use it.

Fortunately, there are two better ways to grab secondary content: `WP_Query` and `get_posts()`. Both do essentially the same thing, but I'll talk about `get_posts()` because it's a little easier to understand.

get_posts() allows us to generate multiple Loops in a single template without changing the page's main query. The only difference is that you'll have to set up your Loop a little differently.

```php
<?php
$custom_posts= get_posts(array('numberposts' => 4,
 →'category'=> 3, orderby => 'title'));
foreach ($custom_posts as $custom_post) :
 →setup_postdata($custom_post); ?>
<h3><?php the_title(); ?></h3>
<?php the_excerpt(); ?>
<?php endforeach; ?>
  ?>
```

You might notice a small change in how you write this Loop versus how you write the Main Loop. That's because the line you used in the Main Loop,

```php
<?php if (have_posts()) : while (have_posts()) :    the_post(); ?>,
```

is reserved for whatever is retrieved from query_posts(), which should be the default information for the page. Instead, get_posts() will return an array of posts that you store in your own variable, which we'll traverse for each Loop.

To use the regular template tags that we've looked at, you call the function setup_postdata(), passing to it the current post information (which is now in the variable $custom_post). Then you proceed as normal, using all of the regular template tags.

Custom Post Types

When Custom Post Types (CPTs) were added to WordPress 3.0, I thought they were the coolest feature add in a while. They really transformed WordPress as a Content Management System (CMS), giving developers the ability to add not only posts and pages, but any kind of content you want.

A CPT is a way for us to add the ability to manage different types of content from within WordPress; each CPT is treated exactly like a post or a page (**Figure 2.5**).

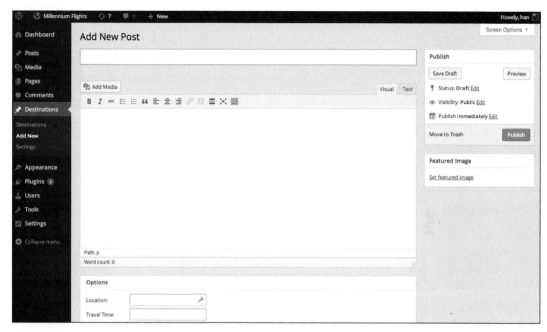

Figure 2.5 The admin for a Destinations Custom Post Type I developed for Millennium Flights. This CPT will list information about the travel destinations offered.

CPTs are based on the way WordPress handles its native post types, of which there are five. Most WordPress users are familiar with posts and pages and can think of them in this way because they are handled similarly. However, there are three other post types:

◆ **Attachments** can be anything uploaded to WordPress using the media uploader, such as images, videos, PDFs, or any other supported file format.

◆ **Revisions** are drafts or different versions of the post.

◆ **Navigation Menus** are the menu items managed through Appearance > Menus in the WordPress admin.

CPTs allow for countless post types; they have been used for business directories, people, real estate listings, courses, homework assignments, and much more. In the example project, we'll be using CPTs for the destinations Millennium Flights travels to.

NOTE
A better name might actually be Custom Content Types, as people tend to think specifically about blog posts when they hear the word "post."

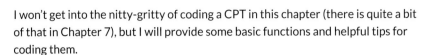

I won't get into the nitty-gritty of coding a CPT in this chapter (there is quite a bit of that in Chapter 7), but I will provide some basic functions and helpful tips for coding them.

The function that will create the Custom Post Type for you is named `register_post_type()`, and it accepts two arguments: a string for post-type, which will also serve as the slug, and an array of arguments for the post type. The arguments are pretty extensive, allowing you to do anything from define the "single label" (e.g., "Destination") to change the menu icon and position. You can read all about them on The WordPress Codex at http://rwdwp.com/15.

If you decide you want to have categories or tags (which fall under the blanket term *taxonomy*), you will do that separate from defining the CPT. Once you register the CPT, you can register new taxonomies and tell WordPress to add them to any of your post types, including custom ones. You would do this using `register_taxonomy()`, which accepts three arguments: a name, an array of post types (listed by slug), and an array of arguments.

When developing CPTs, I would strongly recommend doing the following:

◆ Keep your CPTs in a separate plugin. As discussed earlier, Custom Post Types are patently content. If you add them to a theme (say, via the functions.php file), as soon as you disable that theme, you lose that CPT.

◆ Plan out your CPTs. I usually find it helpful to draw out the fields, what they will map to (e.g., Name > Title), and, most importantly, how each field should be used. It's important to consider text fields versus categories versus tags, for example. If you use the wrong implementation, you may need to hack together a solution or recode the CPT.

◆ If you can, create a simple framework or template for your CPTs. In the resources section of this book, there is a link to mine on GitHub. I've used it for almost all of my CPTs, and it really helps speed up the development process.

Now that you know a bit about CPTs and the fact that they should be in their own plugins, let's talk about creating plugins.

NOTE

A real estate listing CPT might include Title, Description, and photo (all part of the default WordPress editor), as well as additions for price, address, number of bedrooms, number of bathrooms, seller information, number of acres, and more.

Plugins and Shortcodes

Plugins and shortcodes are a great way for users to easily extend functionality without having to know how to code or modify the Core (don't do that), and it's up to us as web developers to make sure the experience with using our plugins is a favorable one. So let's get right into it. Here are the basics of developing a plugin.

A plugin is defined as a program or set of functions that extends the functionality of a WordPress site. It can be anything from a one-liner to a complex set of files that turn WordPress into an e-commerce site. All plugins go into the /wp-content/plugins/ folder, and as long as they are defined properly, they show up in the WordPress admin under the Plugins area (**Figure 2.6**).

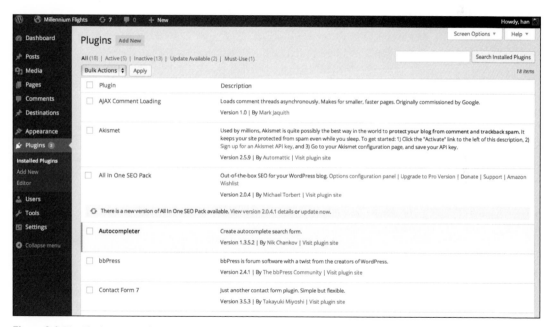

Figure 2.6 The Plugins area of the WordPress admin, where you can enable, disable, add, or remove plugins.

All of your plugin files will exist in a folder that you named within wp-content/ plugins/. It is recommended that you give the folder a unique but informative name so it doesn't conflict with other plugins but is immediately recognizable to users. The same thing goes for the main file, which I generally give the same name as the folder. With the Destinations CPT, I have named the directory /mf-destinations-cpt/ (and similarly, the main file mf-destinations-cpt.php). Just as with functions and classes, I have prefixed my plugin information, which will greatly reduce the chances of a conflict arising. We will be using the prefix mf- for all of our files, folders, functions, classes, and shortcodes.

Within the main file of your plugin directory is the plugin's definition, much like you have a theme definition in the main file of your theme directory:

```
/*
Plugin Name: Destinations CPT
Plugin URI: http://millenniumflights.com
Description: This plugin creates a custom post type & template
→page for all of the Destinations Millennium Flights has
→to offer.
Author: Joe Casabona
Version: 1.0
Author URI: http://casabona.org/
*/
```

You can also include what license is being used (usually it's the GPL), as well as the text of the license, if you'd like.

Once the plugin is defined, you can start coding! There are some conventions developers follow, including everything listed on the WordPress Coding Standards page (http://rwdwp.com/16), which covers a lot of things we've talked about, like using prefixes to avoid conflicts, as well as good coding practices, like sanitizing data before adding it to a database.

The Plugin API allows us to really tap into the power of WordPress by using Hooks, Actions, and Filters.

Hooks, Actions, and Filters

Hooks are pieces of code that allow us to integrate really well with WordPress; there are two types: Actions and Filters.

Actions are functions that are based on some event that is triggered in WordPress. For example, you can add an action that automatically sends a tweet every time you publish a post by using the hook publish_post. Let's say you have an imaginary function called mf_send_tweet(). In your plugin (generally right before or after the function definition), you can add this code:

```
add_action('publish_post', 'mf_send_tweet');
```

This will tell WordPress that as soon as the hook publish_post is triggered, run the function mf_send_tweet(). There is an incredibly long list of hooks for actions, all of which you can find in The Codex at.http://rwdwp.com/17.

Similarly, filters allow us to modify content based on a hook being triggered. Basically, a filter passes some content to the function you specify, you modify that content in some way, then you pass it back for inclusion on the website. For example, let's consider this code:

```
function mf_add_signature($content){
$content .= '<p><img src="'. IMAGES .'/sig.png" alt="Joseph L.
→Casabona, Founder" /></p>';
return $content;
}

add_filter( "the_content", "mf_add_signature" );
```

Here you have a function that will add a signature image to the end of the content that is passed to the function. This is incredibly important: you also *return* that content. If you don't, your filter will not work properly.

With that function defined, you can add a filter with the last line, which calls the function add_filter(). Much like add_action(), you send two arguments: the hook you want, and the function to call when that hook is triggered. You can find a list of all the filters you can use at http://rwdwp.com/18.

About the GPL

In recent years, there was some heated discussion regarding WordPress themes, plugins, developers, and the GPL, which stands for GNU General Public License. This is what makes WordPress open source software. There is also a clause in the GPL that states any files using WordPress' code must also be released under the GPL. That makes any plugins or themes you release would be mostly open source. There is a small loophole, though.

Since CSS and images do not use any WordPress code, they can be released under whatever license you'd like. This caused some conflict between purists, who think entire themes and plugins should be open source, and some developers who were using a dual license: the GPL for WordPress code, and something proprietary for their CSS and images.

WordPress founder Matt Mullenweg has been very vocal about keeping all WordPress related projects completely open source.

Aside from hooks, actions, and filters, you may want to store plugin data for later use. Keep in mind that if you need to store data, there are four ways to do it:

1. Through Custom Post Types, like you are doing with your plugin.

2. Using the WordPress options functions, where you essentially create variables and store them in the wp_options database table. This is recommended for theme options or if you're storing a relatively small amount of data.

3. Custom taxonomies, which you are also employing in your plugin.

4. Creating a database table. In most cases the three above methods should work just fine, but you do have the option to create a database table. If you do create a table, be sure to follow the instructions from The Codex at http://rwdwp.com/19.

Finally, be sure to include shortcodes and template tags for the major functionality of your plugins, and document them. You don't want your users to have to dig through your code to find functionality to add to their themes or pages. Template tags are easy enough; they are simple functions that you allow users to call (which in PHP is any function not explicitly set to private or protected). Users can call those functions in their own plugins or in their themes. You as the developer can then use those template tags to create shortcodes.

Shortcodes

Shortcodes are snippets that users can insert into the WordPress editor to trigger a certain function. Every shortcode will appear in this format: [name_of_shortcode]; WordPress makes creating them incredibly easy. Let's say you have this function:

```
function mf_hello_world(){
    return "Hello World!";
}
```

If you wanted to create a shortcode that would add "Hello World" into a post or a page, all you would need to do is add this somewhere in your plugin (probably either above or below the function definition):

```
add_shortcode('mf_hello', 'mf_hello_world');
```

This would create the shortcode [mf_hello], then call your function when it's placed in the content. One thing you'll notice is that you return rather than print the text you want added. That's because the information returned from the function is what's injected into the content; printing from a shortcode will not work, because the printed material will likely appear in the wrong place.

You can also get pretty advanced with shortcodes, adding in arguments and more. We will see some of that in Chapter 7.

Wrapping Up

Phew! What a chapter! We looked at WordPress themes, CPTs, plugins, shortcodes, and even some bonus content to boot. But we really only just scratched the surface. If you want to get more familiar with WordPress themes, there are some resources listed at the end of the book, including my previous book. Remember—it's important to know the difference between what belongs in a theme and what belongs in a plugin.

I know we didn't get too much into coding, but that's all about to change. In the next few chapters, we are going to develop the theme for Millennium Flights, all along the way making the optimizations WordPress affords us for better responsive design conversion.

Questions

1. What should you ask yourself when determining if code should go in a theme or a plugin?

2. What function should you never use when getting posts for a Loop?

3. What are the five post types built into WordPress?

4. What is the difference between Actions and Filters?

Answers

1. "Would I want to keep this if I redesign the site?"

2. `query_posts()`

3. Posts, pages, revisions, attachments, and navigation menus

4. Actions will trigger some function that should run. Filters will modify the content based on what hook you call.

Chapter **3**

Making Your Theme Responsive: The Ground Floor

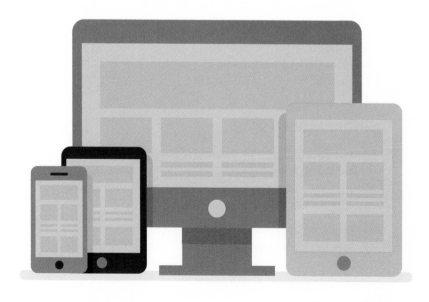

So far we've looked at Responsive Web Design (RWD), its best practices, and some of the core functionality of WordPress, including themes. Now it's time to go through the steps of actually making a responsive theme in WordPress.

The first things we will look at in this chapter are various responsive techniques; we've already explored Media Queries, but there are also Responsive Design + Server Side Components (RESS), JavaScript, and even a built-in WordPress function that will help along the way. Then we'll start the groundwork for our responsive theme.

NOTE

Lazy loading is a longstanding development technique where the program (or in this case, website) will hold off loading something until it's needed.

RESS will allow us to dynamically call snippets of PHP code, HTML, JavaScript, or even entire templates based on the device being used to access the website. There are several techniques to do RESS, including simple User Agent detection—something that WordPress does with a built-in function. There are also several open source techniques; we'll look at the most popular, as well as most accurate, technique.

JavaScript offers a lot of tools designed to improve performance by doing some client-side detections on screen size and device, which can be more accurate than doing it server-side, like in RESS. This includes adding browser support, lazy loading content, and more.

Responsive Techniques

As you can imagine after reading Chapter 1 and the section above, there are a lot of techniques that web developers can employ to create a favorable responsive experience for their users. Though we looked extensively at Media Queries earlier, let's start there.

Media Queries

Media Queries will be at the forefront of your effort to make your WordPress website responsive. By having the ability to control the CSS to update the layout based on screen size, you can create a better, more adaptive experience. But you knew that already, so why talk about it again?

Well, one of the things that makes WordPress so powerful is that for every element it generates, there are associated CSS classes and IDs. You can leverage these to have incredibly fine-grained control over each element on your website. In the upcoming section "Testing WordPress' Default CSS Classes," we'll look at a comprehensive list of these classes and some recommended styles for them.

RESS

RESS emerged a few years after the idea of RWD. The model focuses less on the browser and more on the backend. This technique allowed developers to run server-side device detection and then serve up content based on it. For example, if you have two vastly different navigation methods—one for desktop and one for mobile—you can use RESS to detect the device and serve up the proper navigation.

HOW RESS WORKS

The basic process of RESS is this: You upload a Wireless Universal Resource FiLe (WURFL) to your server, which then gives you access to device/feature detection functions. These functions compare against a database that is constantly updated to include the latest devices.

There aren't many good free/open source WURFLs out there, so we are going to use ScientiaMobile (http://rwdwp.com/20), largely considered to be the best source for devices. You'll see multiple paid options, but you can sign up for a limited free option. There are excellent instructions at http://rwdwp.com/21.

In order to get this sort of device detection up and running:

1. Sign up at ScientiaMobile, and confirm your account.

2. Once your account is confirmed, you will be prompted to generate an API key. Generate the key, and download the PHP Library.

   The capability I selected was `is_wireless_device`. There are several other options, though some require a paid account.

3. Upload the PHP Library to your web server in a folder called /wurfl/.

4. Open /wurfl/examples/MyWurfl.php, and change the variable $api_key to your API key.

5. Navigate to the /wurfl/examples/example.php page on your server. You should see a message regarding the device you're using.

Once you've confirmed that your WURFL library is working, you can work it into your WordPress install. I've added it as a plugin that you can download on GitHub (http:// rwdwp.com/22), but since it's heavily theme dependent, you can also build RESS support right into your theme. Copy the /wurfl/ folder you created earlier into your theme directory. You can delete the /examples/ directory, as you will no longer need it.

NOTE
With Scientia-Mobile's limited free option, you get 5000 device detections per month and a smaller set of detection functions.

Now in your functions.php file, add the following lines:

```
//RESS Goodness
require_once 'wurfl/Client/Client.php';
function mf_is_mobile_device(){
    $config = new WurflCloud_Client_Config();
    $config->api_key = 'YOUR:APIKEY';
    $client = new WurflCloud_Client_Client($config);
$client->detectDevice();
    return $client->getDeviceCapability('is_wireless_device');
}
```

This creates a simple function that will detect a mobile device and return `true` if the device is a smart phone, PDA, or tablet.

WordPress lends itself really well to this sort of "detect and display" method due to its template structure. You can create multiple template files that your theme could call based on RESS results. So imagine you have a mapping like the one shown in **Table 3.1**:

Table 3.1

DESKTOP/FULL WIDTH	MOBILE
sidebar.php	sidebar-mobile.php
menu.php	menu-mobile.php
comments.php	comments-mobile.php

Between RESS and WordPress' template tags (like `get_sidebar()`), building very clean, efficient responsive themes becomes a lot simpler.

WP_IS_MOBILE()

WordPress does have a built-in function to help detect mobile devices called `wp_is_mobile()`, which simply returns `true` if the user is on a mobile device and `false` if not, making it work like any other WordPress Boolean function. This could be a nice alternative if you don't want to pay for a subscription, or as a fallback if you run out of device detections. Instead of using detections for queuing scripts, for example, you could use this function. There is a considerable difference between this and the RESS method mentioned earlier in the chapter.

If you look at the source code for this function, you'll find this:

```
function wp_is_mobile() {
    static $is_mobile;

    if ( isset($is_mobile) )
        return $is_mobile;

    if ( empty($_SERVER['HTTP_USER_AGENT']) ) {
        $is_mobile = false;
    } elseif ( strpos($_SERVER['HTTP_USER_AGENT'], 'Mobile')
    →!== false // many mobile devices (all iPhone, iPad, etc.)
        || strpos($_SERVER['HTTP_USER_AGENT'], 'Android')
            →!== false
        || strpos($_SERVER['HTTP_USER_AGENT'], 'Silk/')
            →!== false
        || strpos($_SERVER['HTTP_USER_AGENT'], 'Kindle')
            →!== false
        || strpos($_SERVER['HTTP_USER_AGENT'], 'BlackBerry')
            →!== false
        || strpos($_SERVER['HTTP_USER_AGENT'], 'Opera Mini')
            →!== false
        || strpos($_SERVER['HTTP_USER_AGENT'], 'Opera Mobi')
            →!== false ) {
            $is_mobile = true;
    } else {
        $is_mobile = false;
    }

    return $is_mobile;
}
```

That's all; what's happening is the function is looking at the browser's User Agent—the string that identifies the type of browser, operating system (OS), and more—and searching for specific browser or OS names associated with mobile devices. This is considerably more primitive than using the WURFL database/ APIs that are available; it only tells us if one of these specific mobile browsers is being used. That said, it can be used in the case that the WURFL database/APIs are inaccessible. Working as a fallback, the mobile detection function from above looks like this:

```php
function mf_is_mobile_device(){
    try{
        $config = new WurflCloud_Client_Config();
        $config->api_key = 'YOUR:APIKEY';
        $client = new WurflCloud_Client_Client($config);
        $client->detectDevice();

        return $client->getDeviceCapability
        →('is_wireless_device');
    }catch (Exception $e){
        return wp_is_mobile();
    }
}
```

Since the WURFL API throws an exception that will show up as PHP errors, we can use a try/catch to hide them from the users, and instead execute the wp_is_mobile() function, providing a nice fallback in case the WURFL API stops working. There is one more line we'll need to add under this function, and that's an execution of the function. Trying to call mf_is_mobile_device() in the templates will result in errors because the WURFL API sends headers and creates cookies, which are not possible once PHP outputs to the browser:

```php
define( 'ISMOBILE', mf_is_mobile_device());
```

This constant, ISMOBILE, is the variable we will use in the rest of the template files.

No matter which method we choose, using RESS we can ensure that certain components are only loaded when they need to be. This should dramatically increase the performance of a site by decreasing the size and amount of unnecessary code loaded. This may really come in handy when you're using the next technique.

JavaScript

It might seem counterintuitive to mention JavaScript at all, considering that Chapter 1 discusses removing unnecessary scripts, especially JavaScripts that add extra bloat. That advice should not be misinterpreted, however. The implication is not that "all JavaScript is bad for mobile." It's quite the contrary, actually; there are a lot of great people developing amazing JavaScript tools to make RWD easier and better. Some of these scripts are:

- **picturefill.js:** A JavaScript polyfill that adds a `<picture>` element to websites. The element allows developers to define several image sources and the minimum screen widths at which to use those images. This is a 1.855KB file that could end up saving users MB of data. Source: http://rwdwp.com/23

- **respond.js:** By default, IE 8 and below do not support the min-width Media Query, making the Mobile First approach difficult; respond.js is a polyfill that will add that support. Source: http://rwdwp.com/24

- **fitvid.js:** A simple jQuery plugin that adds responsive support for videos. Source: http://rwdwp.com/25

- **Responsive Nav:** A simple JavaScript that easily switches navigation from desktop to mobile. This is a pattern we will explore later in this book. Source: http://rwdwp.com/26

These are all lightweight scripts that can be compressed even further and add much more functionality than hassle for the user. As a matter of fact, that is part of a list of considerations you should take into account when deciding whether or not to use JavaScript (or other) plugins. The biggest question you should ask yourself is, "Do I need this?" Are you really improving User Experience (UX), or is this a cool, nice-to-have feature? Is it something that you can use RESS to include only on desktop experiences?

You might also want to consider if it's something you can accomplish with HTML and CSS instead of JavaScript or some other scripting language. Generally speaking, HTML and CSS render much faster than JavaScript, and the browser does not need to make extra HTTP requests.

Finally, consider the file size. Perhaps this function does a lot of really great, helpful things, but if it's 1 MB, it's almost definitely too large. You can also look at "minifying" a file, using such tools as JS Compress (http://rwdwp.com/27). This will remove all white space, extra spaces, and comments, and could dramatically reduce file size.

Moving forward, we are going to explore implementing all three of these technologies into our WordPress themes, starting with adding the responsive layout.

NOTE

A polyfill is simply something added to the browser that isn't there natively. While you can use many languages to implement polyfills, the ones we're going to look at are exclusively JavaScript.

Adding the Responsive Layout

TIP

I actually like
to use a simple
boilerplate theme I
put together, which
you can find here
on GitHub: http://
rwdwp.com/29.

Since this is less a tutorial book and more a presentation of techniques and theories, we won't go through the entire process of creating a WordPress theme; in Chapter 2, we looked extensively at the various parts of the theme and what they mean. Here we'll look at applying the general templates to a blank WordPress theme. The final theme is available on GitHub: http://rwdwp.com/28.

The Millennium Flights HTML Template is available in the same place as the final theme, in a folder called /html/. If you want to follow along, you should download that. The first thing to do (after creating a new folder in the /wp-content/themes/ directory) is add the CSS to your style.css file:

```
/*
Theme Name: Millennium Flights
Theme URI: http://www.millenniumflights.com
Description: A custom theme for Millennium Flights, Inc.
Version: 1.0
Author: Joe Casabona
Author URI: http://www.casabona.org
Tags: blue, white, two-column, flexible-width
*/

/**Normalize.css**/
article,aside,details,figcaption,figure,footer,header,hgroup,
nav,section{display:block}audio,canvas,video{display:
inline-block;*display:inline;*zoom:1}audio:not([controls])
{display:none}[hidden]{display:none}html{font-size:100%;
overflow-y:scroll;-webkit-text-size-adjust:100%;
-ms-text-size-adjust:100%}body{margin:0}body,button,input,
select,textarea{font-family:sans-serif}a{color:#00e}
a:visited{color:#551a8b}a:focus{outline:thin dotted}
a:hover,a:active{outline:0}abbr[title]{border-bottom:1px dotted}
b,strong{font-weight:bold}blockquote{margin:1em 40px}
dfn{font-style:italic}mark{background:#ff0;color:#000}
pre,code,kbd,samp{font-family:monospace,serif;_font-family:
'courier new',monospace;font-size:1em}pre{white-space:pre;
white-space:pre-wrap;word-wrap:break-word}q{quotes:none}q:
```

```
before,q:after{content:'';content:none}small{font-size:75%}
sub,sup{font-size:75%;line-height:0;position:relative;
vertical-align:baseline}sup{top:-0.5em}sub{bottom:-0.25em}
ul,ol{margin:1em 0;padding:0 0 0 40px}dd{margin:0 0 0 40px}
nav ul,nav ol{list-style:none;list-style-image:none}img
{border:0;-ms-interpolation-mode:bicubic}svg:not(:root)
{overflow:hidden}figure{margin:0}form{margin:0}fieldset
{border:1px solid #c0c0c0;margin:0 2px;padding:.35em .625em
.75em}legend{border:0;*margin-left:-7px}button,input,select,
textarea{font-size:100%;margin:0;vertical-align:baseline;
*vertical-align:middle}button,input{line-height:normal}
button,input[type="button"],input[type="reset"],input[type="submit"]
{cursor:pointer;-webkit-appearance:button;*overflow:visible}
input[type="checkbox"],input[type="radio"]{box-sizing:
border-box;padding:0}input[type="search"]{-webkit-appearance:
textfield;-moz-box-sizing:content-box;-webkit-box-sizing:
content-box;box-sizing:content-box}input[type="search"]:
:-webkit-search-decoration{-webkit-appearance:none}button:
:-moz-focus-inner,input::-moz-focus-inner{border:0;padding:0}
textarea{overflow:auto;vertical-align:top}table{border-collapse:
collapse;border-spacing:0}

/** The Crux of the Matter **/

body{
    background: #313C66;
    font-family: "Open Sans Condensed", Helvetica, sans-serif;
    font-size: 62.5%;
    text-align: center;
    color: #FFFFFF;
    }

a, a:visited{
    color: #FFEB73;
    text-decoration: none;
    }
...
```

NOTE
Developers often use CSS resets to "even the playing field" for CSS rendering in all browsers. They'll get rid of any default margin, padding, and other styles found in browsers.

Here you see a snippet of the CSS, starting with the theme definition you saw in Chapter 2. What follows is a minified version of Normalize.css, which is a CSS reset.

Following the reset, you'll see the beginning of the custom CSS for the Millennium Flights theme. What's not shown is all of the CSS that should go in this file, as you'll see in the GitHub repository. That's all you'll need to do for now. In the next section, you'll add styles for default WordPress CSS classes.

The same thing follows for the header, footer, and template files. What you essentially do is replace the static placeholder information with WordPress template tags, which will make the files dynamic. Here, we will look at one example: header. php. In the HTML template, the header is this code:

```
<!DOCTYPE html>
<html lang="en-us">
<head>
        <title>Millennium Flights</title>
        <link rel="stylesheet" href="css/style.css" />
<link href="http://fonts.googleapis.com/css?family=
 →Open+Sans+Condensed:300" rel="stylesheet" type="text/css">
<meta name="viewport" content="width=device-width,
 →initial-scale=1.0" />

<!--[if lt IE 9]>
<script src="http://html5shim.googlecode.com/svn/trunk/
 →html5.js"></script>
<script src="js/respond.min.js"></script>
<![endif]-->
</head>
<body>
        <div id="wrapper">
            <header class="group">
                <h1><img src="images/logo.png"
                 →alt="Millennium Flights" />
                 →Millennium Flights</h1>
                <nav id="main">
                    <ul>
```

```
            <li><a href="#">Home</a></li>
            <li><a href="#">About</a></li>
            <li><a href="#">Destinations</a></li>
            <li><a href="#">Contact</a></li>
        </ul>

    </nav>
</header>

<div id="content" class="group">
```

There are a few areas here that need to be replaced, including the title, style sheet references, and menu. Two areas in particular need attention, however: the JavaScript areas and Google Web Fonts, which should be enqueued instead of just linked directly in the header. That will happen in functions.php.

In the functions.php file on GitHub, you'll find two constants defined for the template path:

```
define( 'TEMPPATH', get_bloginfo('stylesheet_directory'));
define( 'IMAGES', TEMPPATH. "/images");
```

Both of these constants will be used in this section. In the functions.php file, you are going to add this code, which will properly enqueue both the scripts and the Google Web Fonts style sheet:

```
function mf_scripts() {
    wp_enqueue_style( 'googlewebfonts', 'http://fonts.
     →googleapis.com/css?family=Open+Sans+Condensed:300' );
    echo '<!--[if lt IE 9]>';
        echo ' <script src="http://html5shim.googlecode.com/
         →svn/trunk/html5.js"></script>';
        echo ' <script stc="'. TEMPPATH.'/js/respond.min.js">
         →</script>';
        echo '<![endif]-->';

}
```

Here, you have a function that adds your styles and scripts, though there seems to be some inconsistency in how the scripts are loaded. Since there is no way to properly use `wp_enqueue_script()` and use conditional tags, you have to print them manually. This has to be done because those scripts are only needed for IE 8 and below.

After adding that function and replacing the static HTML with template tags, the new header.php file should look like this:

```
<!DOCTYPE html>
<html lang="en-us">
<head>
<title><?php bloginfo('name'); ?> | <?php wp_title(); ?>
 →</title>
<link rel="stylesheet" href="<?php bloginfo('stylesheet_url');
 →?>" type="text/css" media="screen" />
<link rel="pingback" href="<?php bloginfo('pingback_url');
 →?>" />

<?php wp_head(); ?>

</head>
<body>
    <div id="wrapper">
        <header class="group">
            <h1><img src="<?php print IMAGES;?>/logo.png"
                →alt="<?php bloginfo('name'); ?>" />
                →<?php bloginfo('name'); ?></h1>
            <nav id="main">
                <?php wp_nav_menu( array('menu' => 'Main' )); ?>
            </nav>
        </header>

        <div id="content" class="group">
```

There you have it! As we move through the rest of the book, we will look at specific sections of the theme and how to make them nice and responsive using a combination of the techniques we looked at earlier. Let's continue by looking at WordPress' default CSS classes.

Testing WordPress' Default CSS Classes

In order to make themes as flexible as possible, when WordPress generates markup it includes several CSS classes that can be styled by developers. Some of the classes can be removed on the theme level; these are classes generated by functions like `body_class()` and `post_class()`. Some, however, are generated by the WordPress editor and cannot be removed (at least not without some hacking). Those classes are: `.entry-content img`, `.alignleft`, `img.alignleft`, `.alignright`, `img.alignright`, `.aligncenter`, `img.aligncenter`, `.alignnone`, `img.alignnone`, `.wp-caption`, `.wp-caption img`, `.wp-caption`, `p.wp-caption-text`, `.wp-smiley`, `.gallery dl`, `.gallery dt`, `.gallery dd`, `.gallery dl a`, `.gallery dl img`, `.gallery-caption`, `.size-full`, `.size-large`, `.size-medium`, `.size-thumbnail`.

Most of these are self-explanatory; `.alignleft` and `.alignright` are classes to align text or images left or right. The default styles for these should be something like this:

```
.alignleft, img.alignleft {
    display: inline;
    float: left;
    text-align: left;
    margin: 0 1% 0 0;
    }
.alignright, img.alignright {
    display: inline;
    float: right;
    text-align: right;
    margin: 0 0 0 1%;
    }
```

This will ensure that elements that are assigned these classes will display as WordPress users expect them to.

Then there are classes like `.wp-caption` that give you a bit more freedom in how you might want to display them. Following is a list of default styles that are used in the Millennium Flights theme (before any media queries are defined):

```css
.wp-caption, .alignleft, img.alignleft, .alignright, img.
alignright, .aligncenter,div.aligncenter {
    display: block;
    margin-left: auto;
    margin-right: auto;
    }

.wp-caption, .aligncenter{
    border: 1px solid #ddd;
    text-align: center;
    background-color: #f3f3f3;
    padding: 0.4em;
    }

.wp-caption img {
    margin: 0;
    padding: 0;
    border: 0 none;
    }

.wp-caption p.wp-caption-text {
    font-size: 0.85em;
    line-height: 1.1em;
    padding: 0 0.4em 0.4em;
    margin: 0;
    color: #333333;
    }
```

There are some pretty simple styles here just to give the images and captions some formatting. Everything is more or less formatted as a centered block. It's not until the layout widens that the images/classes actually align left or right.

```
@media screen and (min-width: 34.188em){

    .aligncenter, div.aligncenter {
        display: block;
        margin-left: auto;
        margin-right: auto;
        }

    .alignleft, img.alignleft{
        float: left;
        max-width: 40%;
        text-align: left;
        margin: 0 1% 0 0;
        }

    .alignright, img.alignright{
        float: right;
        max-width: 40%;
        text-align: right;
        margin-left: 0 0 0 1%;
        }

    .wp-caption, img.alignleft, img.alignright, .aligncenter{
        border: 1px solid #ddd;
        text-align: center;
        background-color: #f3f3f3;
        padding-top: 4px;
        }

    .wp-caption img {
        margin: 0;
        padding: 0;
        border: 0 none;
        }
```

```
.wp-caption p.wp-caption-text {
    font-size: 0.85em;
    line-height: 1.1em;
    padding: 0 0.4em 0.4em;
    margin: 0;
    }
}
```

As the layout expands, it makes sense to apply floating styles to the `.alignleft` and `.alignright` classes. You might also notice that the width of the images is limited to 40%. An assumption is made here that if the user is aligning the image to one side, it should not expand the full width of the content area. Limiting it to 40% ensures that it doesn't get too wide; you don't want to have a situation where the block is primarily an image with a small sliver of text, as shown in **Figure 3.1**.

Figure 3.1 You don't want to have a situation where the image leaves room for just a sliver of text.

Photo by Philip J. Casabona

As you expand out further, you can get more fine-grained with the widths, eventually allowing for images to display at their full width once the screen is wide enough.

The other styles listed above, including gallery and specific image size styles, don't necessarily need default styles, as the ones listed here will handle them, at least partially. In Chapter 7, we will explore making WordPress' default gallery responsive.

Comments and Widgets

Aside from handling classes applied in the editor, WordPress automatically generates classes for comments and widgets. We will look at both of these specifically in Chapter 4, but for reference, here is an image showing a WordPress comment, with some of the default classes applied (**Figure 3.2**).

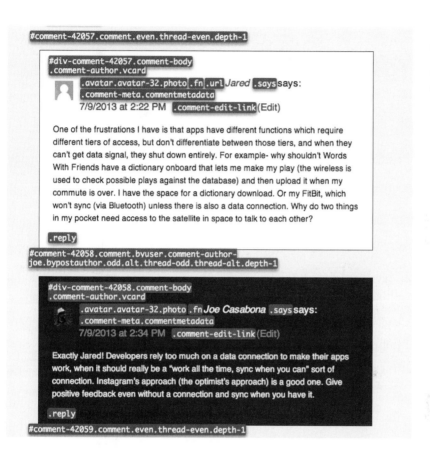

Figure 3.2 There are quite a few styles automatically generated for comments to control almost every element.

As you can see, there are a lot of styles associated with comments, and that's not even the entire list. To get a better idea of how much control you have, here are all the styles:

```
.commentlist .reply {}
.commentlist .reply a {}
.commentlist .alt {}
.commentlist .odd {}
.commentlist .even {}
.commentlist .thread-alt {}
.commentlist .thread-odd {}
.commentlist .thread-even {}
.commentlist li ul.children .alt {}
.commentlist li ul.children .odd {}
```

```
.commentlist li ul.children .even {}
.commentlist .vcard {}
.commentlist .vcard cite.fn {}
.commentlist .vcard span.says {}
.commentlist .vcard img.photo {}
.commentlist .vcard img.avatar {}
.commentlist .vcard cite.fn a.url {}
.commentlist .comment-meta {}
.commentlist .comment-meta a {}
.commentlist .commentmetadata {}
.commentlist .commentmetadata a {}
.commentlist .parent {}
.commentlist .comment {}
.commentlist .children {}
.commentlist .pingback {}
.commentlist .bypostauthor {}
.commentlist .comment-author {}
.commentlist .comment-author-admin {}
.commentlist {}
.commentlist li {}
.commentlist li p {}
.commentlist li ul {}
.commentlist li ul.children li {}
.commentlist li ul.children li.alt {}
.commentlist li ul.children li.byuser {}
.commentlist li ul.children li.comment {}
.commentlist li ul.children li.depth-{id} {}
.commentlist li ul.children li.bypostauthor {}
.commentlist li ul.children li.comment-author-admin {}
#cancel-comment-reply {}
#cancel-comment-reply a {}
```

We might not make use of all of these explicitly, but in Chapter 4 we'll make the most of what's given to us.

As for widgets, WordPress has several default/stock widgets that all come with their own styles. A vanilla WordPress install includes the widgets shown in **Figure 3.3**.

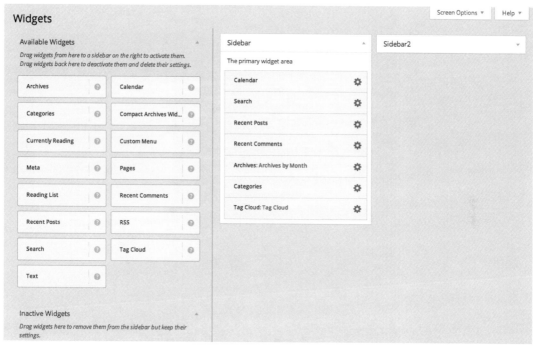

Figure 3.3 A list of all the default WordPress widgets.

All of these have their own classes associated with them, and the blog Digging into WordPress has a nice list of them here: http://rwdwp.com/30.

We could probably cover an entire chapter on responsive WordPress widgets if we look at each of these individually. The truth is that we can cut out a lot of code by using widget containers, the proper selectors, and general CSS. In functions. php for the Millennium Flights theme, there is a sidebar registered that includes container information:

TIP
Digging into WordPress has an extensive list of all of the default styles here: http://rwdwp. com/31.

```
register_sidebar( array (
    'name' => __( 'Sidebar', 'main-sidebar' ),
    'id' => 'primary-widget-area',
    'description' => __( 'The primary widget area', 'mf' ),
    'before_widget' => '<div class="widget">',
    'after_widget' => '</div>',
    'before_title' => '<h3 class="widget-title">',
    'after_title' => '</h3>'
) );
```

The Calendar Widget

The Calendar widget in WordPress, which displays a calendar view of your posts, is represented as a table. While on a greater scale this could cause problems, this particular table is small enough that it shouldn't cause layout issues. One possible improvement could be increasing the size of the numbers to make it easier for mobile users to press.

Figure 3.4 The WordPress Calendar widget displays a list of your posts by date.

The best way to handle the CSS for all widgets is to style the `.widget` container, applying the same styles to all widgets listed for that sidebar. If you decide in your theme that specific styles are needed for a particular widget, you can use the guide above or your favorite browser extension to determine which styles need to be adjusted. One piece of advice: Be mindful of how forms display in the sidebar. For instance, it would be wise to make sure the search widget doesn't get too large by applying the CSS from the outset:

```
.searchform {
    max-width: 98%;
    }
input.search {
    max-width: 98%;
    }
```

Regarding the search form, you can also change how the form is generated using the searchform.php template.

We will look more at styling responsive widgets in Chapter 4.

Miscellaneous Styles

We've already looked at a lot of classes, but it turns out there are a lot more. WordPress pumps out special classes for almost every element that it generates, including body text, post areas, category/taxonomy classes, and much, much more. Luckily, you don't need to add default CSS for these classes, and you can choose to remove some of them throughout theme development.

There are several ways you can take advantage of them however. Using `body_class()` or `post_class()` means that you can apply styles to specific pages or even posts, as classes like `.<page-name>` or `.post-<id>` are generated. Perhaps you have a special post or guide that might work better when different CSS are applied to it. Between using these generated classes, Media Queries, and even RESS, you can develop really nice custom post layouts.

If you're concerned about creating unused or extra markup, you could always remove the template tags and replace them with your own homegrown class structure, like so:

```
<body class="<?php print 'page-'.get_the_ID(); ?>">
<div class="post <?php print 'post-'.get_the_ID(); ?>">
```

Beware, though. If you do this, it can lead to a lot of unnecessary headache (pain, suffering, the dark side, etc). Developers only really need to do this on high-traffic sites, where everything needs to be optimized.

NOTE

One concern some developers may have is that adding classes that are not used creates extra, unnecessary markup. I would say that the amount of extra markup is trivial.

Wrapping Up

Media Queries, RESS, and JavaScript are at the heart of what we will accomplish in the coming chapters, where we'll apply the techniques and theories we've talked about. Media Queries will help us adapt our layout to the user's screen, RESS will allow us to conditionally call sections of the template based on the user's device, and JavaScript will provide tools for fallbacks, polyfills, and changing HTML on the fly.

Bringing a responsive template into WordPress is an initially intuitive task; just copy the CSS and HTML, and replace the static areas with dynamic code like template tags or the Loop. As you'll see moving forward, though, the process might not be as clear-cut as it seems. In this chapter, we added some code to properly handle adding JavaScript and extra style sheets, but more should be done in this regard; we will look at what else we can do in the following chapters.

Finally, WordPress has a ton of default classes that are generated when a site is created. Some, like `.alignleft`, `.alignright`, and `.wp-caption`, are generated from the editor and should always get default styles. Other areas, like comments and widgets, are controlled in some fashion by the theme designer, but should not be ignored. In Chapter 4, we will explore ways to properly display and load these elements so they don't burden the user.

Questions

1. What does RESS stand for, and what does it do?

2. What is a WURFL file/database?

3. What is the built-in RESS-like WordPress function? How is it different from a WURFL database?

4. What is the number-one question you should ask yourself when considering the inclusion of a JavaScript file?

Answers

1. RESS stands for Responsive Design + Server Side Components. It allows you to detect the type of device on the server level, giving you the option to include (or exclude) certain template elements based on the results.

2. WURFL stands for Wireless Universal Resource FiLe. It is used in RESS to detect devices and capabilities.

3. The built-in RESS-like WordPress function is `wp_is_mobile()`. It differs from WURFL databases because it only tells us which specific browser/OS is being used. It can be used as a fallback if the WURFL file is inaccessible.

4. "Do I need this?" If you don't, the extra files probably aren't worth it for the user to download.

Chapter

Making Your Theme Responsive: Core Features

So far, you've seen multiple ways to make a website responsive. Now it's time to really dig in and combine those techniques with WordPress' unique capabilities.

In Chapter 3, you learned how to apply your responsive CSS to a WordPress theme. You also got an in-depth look at WordPress' generated CSS classes and created some default styles for what are considered the "essential" ones. From here on out, you'll go even further, focusing on two types of features: core and blog.

This chapter looks at some of the core features of WordPress instrumental to a good User Experience. The next chapters are about using what WordPress provides developers and leveraging those tools to create better responsive sites. That said, you'll look at three areas of development in this chapter: navigation menus, images, and widgets.

Handling Navigation

Responsive navigation techniques are bountiful in books and blog posts; many developers have come up with their own implementations for navigation menus on responsive sites. Brad Frost outlines some of the most popular ones at http://rwdwp.com/32.

In this section, we will look at a few popular techniques and how they look on the Millennium Flights site, and then decide what's best.

A Look at Popular Techniques

If you looked at Brad Frost's post, you'll see that he also wrote a second one and linked to several others. In other words, there are lots of navigation menu patterns to choose from.

We will explore three possible options for the Millennium Flights navigation: Do Nothing (or Top Nav), Jump to (or Footer nav), and the Select box...plus a bonus technique that may surprise you. While we won't be implementing it, we will also look at the Off-Canvas technique, which is a bit more advanced

DO NOTHING (OR TOP NAV)

This is the easiest one to implement. You simply leave the navigation as is at the top of your site; you'll see what the "technique" looks like in **Figure 4.1**.

"Hide and Cry"

Frost mentions one technique in which you hide your navigation from mobile users, naming it "Hide and Cry." This reflects the all-too-prevalent thinking that users on mobile don't need as much functionality as those on the desktop, and it's wrong. 31% of American adults in 2012 used their phones for the majority of their Internet access. In essence, you're punishing mobile users by limiting their experience and making them download content that they'll never see. It might be a convenient way to handle other pages—saving on page height and adjusting the navigation—but it's a bad practice, for some of the reasons discussed in Chapter 1, primarily that you make users download sections of websites they will never see, increasing bandwidth required to download the site and slowing things down.

Figure 4.1 Millennium Flights with the "Do Nothing" responsive navigation technique.

As long as your navigation styles are not limited by a specific Media Query, they will apply to the entire site if you employ the Do Nothing technique. It is easy to apply because you don't have to make changes to your code, but there are some pitfalls. Luckily the navigation for Millennium Flights uses big text, but imagine a site with smaller text using this approach. Users may have difficulty selecting the menu items on smaller screens (**Figure 4.2**).

Figure 4.2 On the left is how this website navigation renders on an Android phone. On the right, you see what happens when you resize the browser. In both cases, the nav appears small and difficult to press without zooming.

The other big issue with the technique is that as a user adds more menu items, the height of the page increases. You don't want to have a situation where the user only sees a logo and menu items on page load on a smart phone.

"DO SOME THINGS"

I have a slight modification to this approach, which I've very cleverly called "Do Some Things." It's the idea that functionally, nothing about the navigation changes; it doesn't change locations or implementations. It's still an unordered list at the top of the page. That is, it will stay in the same place and it will be a list of menu items, exactly the same on both layouts. However, you do make slight tweaks and changes to the CSS, optimizing it a little bit for mobile. An example can be seen on my personal site, Casabona.org (**Figure 4.3**).

Figure 4.3 Casabona.org's navigation on both mobile and desktop layouts. The position of the navigation doesn't change, but the items become more button-like on mobile to make pressing them easier for the user.

NOTE
It should be mentioned that this section isn't going to present a single "right" approach; it all depends on the situation. These are just the options.

Not too much has changed in the overall webpage layout, but you'll see each menu item on smaller screens is its own individual button (as opposed to the contiguous grey bar on wider screens), and the font gets a little bolder on smaller screens.

This slightly modified approach still runs into some of the pitfalls of the "Do Nothing" approach, like taking up a lot of screen real estate on small screens.

JUMP TO OR FOOTER ANCHOR

In this technique, as the screen gets smaller, the navigation is replaced by a single link that jumps the user to navigation in the footer. This, like the "Do Nothing" approach, is easy to implement, but it saves on screen real estate, as the menu is no longer at the top to take up space (**Figure 4.4**).

Figure 4.4 The Jump to navigation. The menu items are replaced with a single link that brings users to the bottom of the page.

There are a couple of ways to code this technique. The most common one is to use CSS's display: none; to hide the navigations that should not be in use. For example, if this is the header and footer markup:

Header Markup

```
<nav id="main">
<div class="full">
        <?php wp_nav_menu( array('menu' => 'Main' )); ?>
    </div>
    <div class="jump">
        <a href="#footernav">Jump to Nav</a>
    </div>
</nav>
```

Footer Markup

```
<nav id="footernav">
    <?php wp_nav_menu( array('menu' => 'Main' )); ?>
</nav>
```

The CSS would look like this:

```
nav#main .full{ display: none; }

#footernav ul{
    margin: 0;
    padding: 0;
    }

#footernav li{
    font-size: 1.5em;
```

```
        border-bottom: 1px solid #FFFFFF;
        }

#footernav li a{
    padding: 10px;
    }

...
@media screen and (min-width: 34.188em){

...

nav#main .full{
    display: block;
    }
#footernav, nav#main .jump{
    display: none;
    }

...
}
```

This code works fine, but it's forcing the user to download code that he isn't going to see. Later in this section, you are going to see how this method can be improved using RESS.

Aside from the extra code, this experience might be a jarring one for the user. The page view would change from the top of the page to the bottom without any scrolling or animations, changing everything the user was looking at; it's not very smooth. A better solution, and one that takes into account the issues we've seen with the techniques we've looked at, would be to convert the navigation to a Select box for mobile.

THE SELECT BOX

The Select box is a clean, user-friendly method that places the navigation at the top of the page without taking up too much screen space. One drawback is that it's not as easy to implement as the previous methods because you actually need to code up two separate menus—one normal menu, and one inside of a select box (**Figure 4.5**).

Adding Smooth Scrolling to the "Jump to" Technique

You can make the transition a bit smoother using a jQuery scroll effect. After adding jQuery, add this function to your header (or functions.php using the wp_head action):

```javascript
$(function() {
  $('a[href*=#]:not([href=#])').click(function() {
    if (location.pathname.replace(/^\//,'') ==
    →this.pathname.replace(/^\//,'')
        || location.hostname == this.hostname) {
      var target = $(this.hash);
      target = target.length ? target : $('[name=' +
      →this.hash.slice(1) +']');
      if (target.length) {
        $('html,body').animate({
          scrollTop: target.offset().top
        }, 1000);
        return false;
      }
    }
  });
});
```

Figure 4.5 The Select box navigation approach clears up a lot of room while still keeping navigation at the top; however, the user still has to download two different navigation menus.

Let's think outside of WordPress for a second, and look at the HTML structure for a select menu navigation:

```
<select onchange="location=this.options[this.selectedIndex].
→value;">
    <option value="" selected="selected">Go to...</option>
    <option value="/home/">Home</option>
    <option value="/about/">About</option>
    <option value="/destinations/">Destinations</option>
    <option value="/contact/">Contact</option>
</select>
```

While this seems like a pretty standard implementation, it's actually going to take a little bit of work to get this properly working in WordPress because it changes the entire structure of the menu. Luckily, WordPress allows developers to do just that with the Walker_Nav_Menu class. A "Walker" in programming is a way to traverse, or process, tree-like data structures, which create hierarchical data. In this case, it's traversing HTML to create an unordered list of nav items. You will create a file called Select_Nav_Walker.php, where you will write a class that extends Walker_Nav_Menu, using the four functions it uses to display the menu:

```
class Select_Nav_Walker extends Walker_Nav_Menu {

    public function start_lvl(&$output, $depth){}
    public function end_lvl(&$output, $depth){}
    public function start_el(&$output, $item, $depth, $args){}
    public function end_el(&$output, $item, $depth){}
}
```

The functions start_lvl and end_lvl print the opening and closing elements for the menu; by default this is <ul> and </ul>. You will actually add the new markup (the <select> tags from above) in a different area, so both of those functions will remain as is: blank.

The other two functions, start_el and end_el, will be used to print the individual menu items. end_el is incredibly simple:

```
public function end_el(&$output, $item, $depth){
    $output .= "</option>\n";
}
```

The function is just one line—the markup that closes the menu item. By default, it is </li>, but since this is a select menu, you are changing it to </option>. The variable $output is what this class continually adds to before sending it back to be printed on the screen. Because of that, it's important to use ".=" and not just "=". If you don't, your menu will just be </option>.

The start_el function is a little more complicated than that, and it will make use of the $item argument passed to it:

```
public function start_el(&$output, $item, $depth, $args){
    $item->title = esc_attr($item->title);
    parent::start_el(&$output, $item, $depth, $args);
    $output .= '    <option value="'. $item->url .'">'.
    →$item->title;
}
```

The first line escapes the title, converting special characters to HTML entities. Then it calls the parent function (remember this class is extending the built-in Walker_Nav_Menu class), which will apply all CSS classes that would otherwise be applied. Finally, we send the <option> element to $output. $item is an array that has several values, including url and title.

That completes the class, with the entire thing looking like this:

```
class Select_Nav_Walker extends Walker_Nav_Menu {

    public function start_lvl(&$output, $depth){}

    public function end_lvl(&$output, $depth){}

    public function start_el(&$output, $item, $depth, $args){
        $item->title = esc_attr($item->title);
        parent::start_el(&$output, $item, $depth, $args);
        $output .= '    <option value="'. $item->url .'">'.
        →$item->title;
    }

    public function end_el(&$output, $item, $depth){
        $output .= "</option>\n";
    }
}
```

You can either place it directly into functions.php or in its own file, including it in functions.php.

After that, you'll need to attend to the header.php markup, which looks like this:

```
<nav id="main">
<div class="full">
        <?php wp_nav_menu( array('menu' => 'Main' )); ?>
    </div>
    <div class="select-menu">
        <?php
            wp_nav_menu(array(
                'menu' => 'Main',
                'walker'           => new Select_Nav_Walker(),
                'items_wrap'       => '<select ONCHANGE=
                →"location=this.options[this.selectedIndex].
                →value;"><option>Go to..</option>%3$s</select>',
                'container' => false
                )
            );
        ?>
    </div>
</nav>
```

You will show/hide the proper menu the same way you did with the Footer Anchor technique, but we will explore a better option later in this section.

What should be pointed out here are the new entries for the select-menu version of wp_nav_menu(). There are three new arguments being passed to it:

◆ walker: The value of the Walker is the instantiation of your Select_Nav_Walker class. This tells WordPress to use this walker instead of the default to construct the menu.

◆ items_wrap: By default, this is the <ul> wrapper for the normal walker. Since your walker is for a select menu, the appropriate markup should be sent. You'll also notice the %3$s. This is necessary to make sure $output is included.

◆ container: This by default wraps the entire list in a div, which we don't need to do.

That's everything. Now you should have the regular menu at full width and the select menu for smaller screens. This still has the issue of multiple menus being downloaded, but we will fix that later.

OFF CANVAS

This technique is by far the most advanced one we'll cover, but it's also the slickest. With this method, you'll have your main content on screen and then a button (or even swipe) to reveal more content off to the left or right. This is used by a lot of mobile applications to place the navigation on the left side, hidden away (**Figure 4.6**).

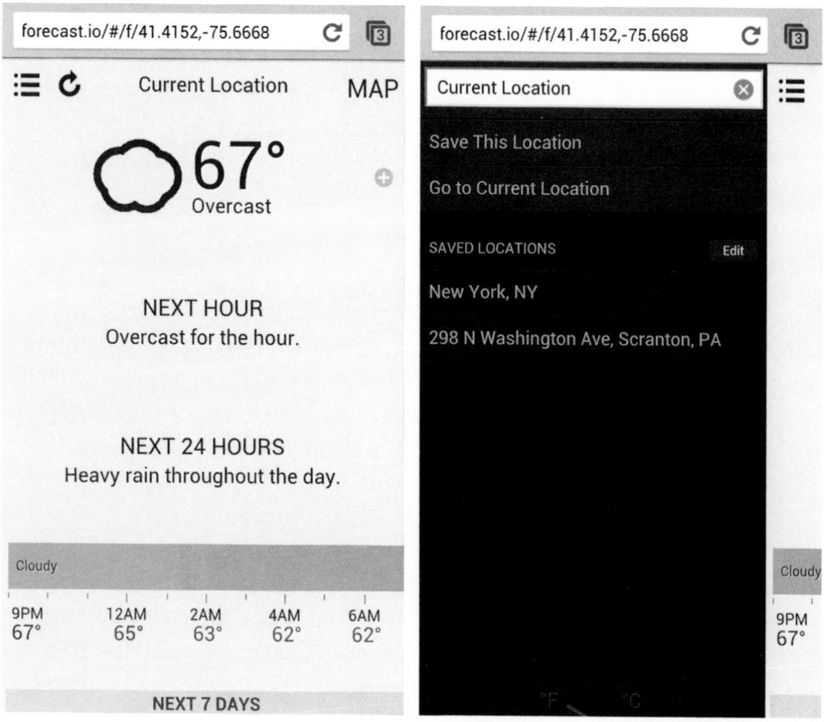

TIP
There are WordPress plugins that achieve this same effect. It seems the most popular one is this one: http://rwdwp.com/33.

Figure 4.6 Forecast.io, an incredible mobile website, employs the off canvas technique.

This technique completely frees up screen space so the user only sees content. The biggest drawback is the difficulty in implementing it. Depending on how you do it, you could be hiding content, and you will almost definitely use JavaScript (probably jQuery) for the animation effect. It would also, in essence, create an entirely new page section you would have to manage. If you want to see this technique in action or take a crack at it yourself, Jason Weaver and Luke Wroblewski have released code, resources, and examples at http://rwdwp. com/34 (**Figure 4.7**).

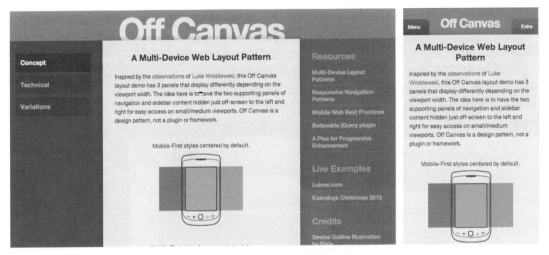

Figure 4.7 The Off Canvas website has a live demo, sample code, and resources for those interested in trying it out.

This is not the only implementation of the off canvas approach. If menus (or any content) slide down from the top or up from the bottom, it's also considered off canvas, which is really just the viewable area on the screen. Due to its popularity, an open source JavaScript plugin was created to easily implement it. It's called responsive-nav.js. Let's look at implementing that into the Millennium Flights theme.

RESPONSIVE-NAV.JS

In Chapter 3, we saw some questions that should be asked when considering using some piece of JavaScript; questions like, "Do I need this?" and "How large is the file?" Truth be told, we really don't *need* to use responsive-nav.js. However, it is one of the best and most lightweight implementations of the off canvas approach out there. At 1.7 KB, it's considered small by anyone's standard.

Everything you'll need to implement this can be found at http://rwdwp.com/26 (**Figure 4.8**).

Figure 4.8
The Responsive Nav
home page, illustrating
how the JavaScript
works.

A few things need to happen in order to make responsive-nav.js work in the
Millennium Flights theme. First, you'll need to enqueue the script (after downloading the files). Since there is already a function to do that in the theme, you can
just add a new line to it:

```
function mf_scripts() {
    wp_enqueue_style( 'googlewebfonts',
    →'http://fonts.googleapis.com/css?family=
    →Open+Sans+Condensed:300' );
    wp_enqueue_script( 'responsivenav',
    →TEMPPATH.'/js/responsive-nav.min.js', array());
    echo '<!--[if lt IE 9]>';
    echo '<script src="http://html5shim.googlecode.com/
    →svn/trunk/html5.js"></script>';
    echo '<script src="'. TEMPPATH .'/js/respond.min.js">
    →</script>';
    echo '![endif]-->';

}
```

Since the script requires the containing div to have a CSS ID, you'll have to modify the nav function slightly. In header.php, change the wp_nav_menu function to this:

```
<nav id="main">
<?php wp_nav_menu( array('menu' => 'Main',
→'container_id' => 'top-menu')); ?>
</nav>
```

You're adding one more argument, container_id, which will add id="top-menu" to the div containing the nav menu. Then it's time to add the CSS.

From the downloaded files, you'll also find a style sheet called responsive-nav. css. You can copy that CSS into your theme's style.css file, but you'll need to make some modifications. This will go before any Media Queries:

```
#top-menu ul {
    margin: 0;
    padding: 0;
    width: 100%;
    display: block;
    list-style: none;
    }

#top-menu li {
    width: 100%;
    }

.js #top-menu {
    clip: rect(0 0 0 0);
    max-height: 0;
    position: absolute;
    display: block;
    overflow: hidden;
    zoom: 1;
    }
```

```
nav.opened {
    max-height: 9999px;
    }
```

This is a slight modification of the default CSS, changed only to match our new menu selector. The same thing goes for the CSS added after the first Media Query:

```
@media screen and (min-width: 34.188em){
    .js #top-menu {
        position: relative;
        }
    .js #top-menu {
        max-height: none;
        }
    #nav-toggle {
        display: none;
        }
    ...
    }
```

Finally, there is a bit of JavaScript that should go before the </body> tag. To insert it into the theme, we can use the wp_footer action:

```
function mf_responsive_nav(){
echo '<script>
            var navigation = responsiveNav("#top-menu");
        </script>';
}

add_action('wp_footer', 'mf_responsive_nav');
```

This will tell responsive-nav.js to look for the div with the ID top-menu and apply the changes to the menu in that container. Once that is done, you should be able to refresh your page and see the results (**Figure 4.9**).

Figure 4.9 Millennium Flights with the default settings for responsive-nav.js. Most of what's seen here is customizable through JavaScript or CSS.

Most of what can be seen in the screenshot is customizable using CSS or the arguments you pass to the responsiveNav() function. In the final version of the theme, instead of the text, "Menu," the common menu icon (often called the "hamburger" for some unfortunate reason) is used.

Changing Navigation on the Server Side

Up until this point, the techniques you've been using relied completely on CSS—namely showing and hiding navigation based on breakpoints. However, in Chapter 3, you saw a function that could be especially helpful for navigation: mf_is_mobile_device(). Using this, you can choose to conditionally show one version of the site's navigation over another instead of loading both. Let's first look at the select box navigation. Instead of having this:

```
<nav id="main">
<div class="full">
        <?php wp_nav_menu( array('menu' => 'Main' )); ?>
    </div>
    <div class="select-menu">
        <?php
            wp_nav_menu(array(
                'menu' => 'Main',
                'walker'        => new Select_Nav_Walker(),
                'items_wrap'    => '<select ONCHANGE=
                →"location=this.options[this.selectedIndex].
                →value;"><option>Go to..</option>%3$s</select>',
                'container' => false
                )
            );
        ?>
    </div>
</nav>
```

...we can have something much cleaner, and requiring much less CSS:

```
<nav id="main">
<?php
if(!ISMOBILE){
        wp_nav_menu( array('menu' => 'Main', 'container_id' =>
        →'top-menu'));
    }else{
        wp_nav_menu(array(
            'menu' => 'Main',
            'walker'        => new Select_Nav_Walker(),
            'items_wrap'    => '<select ONCHANGE=
            →"location=this.options[this.selectedIndex].
            →value;"><option>Go to..</option>%3$s</select>',
            'container' => false
            )
        );
    }
?>
</nav>
```

Notice there isn't an extra class to hide one menu over the other. It simply says, "If the user is not on a mobile device, print the normal menu. Otherwise, print the select box menu." This means the user isn't downloading two sets of navigation, and you don't have to write extra CSS to hide or show that navigation based on breakpoints.

The same thing can be done with the Jump to or Footer Anchor approach. In header.php, you'll have:

```
<nav id="main">
<?php
    if(!ISMOBILE){
        wp_nav_menu( array('menu' => 'Main',
        →'container_id' => 'top-menu'));
    }else{
        echo '<a href="#footernav">Jump to Nav</a>';
    }
?>
</nav>
```

NOTE

When testing a layout using RESS, you won't be able to just resize your browser window; you will have to do device testing.

This is constructed just like the Select box code above, except there is a jump link to the footer. And here is what the footer.php markup looks like:

```php
<?php if(ISMOBILE){ ?>
<nav id="footernav">
        <?php wp_nav_menu( array('menu' => 'Main' )); ?>
    </nav>
<?php } ?>
```

TIP

If you are having issues implementing RESS into your theme or need some added functionality, Jesse Friedman's WP Mobile Detect plugin is available in the Plugin Repository http://rwdwp. com/35.

In the footer, you are checking to make sure the user is on a mobile device before printing out the navigation.

Moving forward, we will be able to employ this technique in several other areas of the theme. So with all of these techniques and more, how do you decide which one to use?

Ask What's Best for the Users

As with just about anything in the field of web development (nay, design and development in general), it's best to ask what's best for your users. In many cases, that might be whatever takes up the least amount of screen real estate.

However, maybe your users would understand the navigation better if they saw it all laid out in front of them. Maybe your users don't realize what the "hamburger" icon is. The best thing to do is some research into how your users use your website. Do some A/B testing, or at the very least, get the opinion of friends and family. Ask your users for feedback. As with a lot of things in coding, simple is probably better than clever.

To determine what's best for your users, ask yourself a few questions:

◆ From what class/type of devices do my users access the site?

◆ Are my users there to see what's on the home page, or do they usually go to a different page?

◆ What information do *I* want to present as most important?

◆ How tech-savvy are my users?

And, as mentioned earlier, give them some options and see what works out best.

Using SVG Images

We won't discuss Scalable Vector Graphics (SVG) extensively here because it's not specific to WordPress, but it is a very good technique to use when it comes to scalable images. SVGs have no set pixel widths or heights associated with them (though there is a default width and height). Because of this, they scale well without losing quality, and even look great on Apple Retina displays.

Using them is as easy as using the `<img>` tag, though there are some support issues, namely for IE 8 and below and Android 2.3 and below. Chris Coyier has a really great tutorial for getting started here: http://rwdwp.com/36. In order to allow SVG uploads in WordPress, you will also need this function (also courtesy of Chris Coyier):

```
function mf_allow_svg( $mimes ){
    $mimes['svg'] = 'image/svg+xml';
    return $mimes;
}
add_filter( 'upload_mimes', 'mf_allow_svg' );
```

Handling Images

Images are one of the biggest sticking points for making a website truly responsive; it's not good enough to just resize them along with the layout or container. There are a lot of tools and techniques out there to aid in better resizing, smaller file sizes, faster loading, and more. What really helps is the way WordPress processes uploaded images.

How WordPress Uploads Images

By default, when you upload an image, the WordPress media uploader creates several different sizes: thumbnail (150x150px max), medium (300x300px max), large (1024x1024px max), and full, which is the original size of the uploaded image. You can also specify different sizes using `the_post_thumbnail()` or `get_the_post_thumbnail()`, but this will only return an `<img>` tag with width and height specified. If you want just an image URL, you can use `wp_get_attachment_image_src()`, which returns an array with URL, width, height, and a Boolean; the Boolean tells you if the image is a resized version (true) or the original (false).

TIP
This is also really
useful if you want
to create a more di-
verse image range
for the technique
we are going to
implement in the
next section.

You can add new image sizes associated with keywords like "thumbnail," or "medium," for example, which will get resized. That function is `add_image_size()`; if you want to create a feature Destination image for the Millennium Flights CPT, you would use this code:

```
add_image_size('mf_destinations_featured', 650, 300, true);
```

In order, the parameters are: $name (which can be used in functions like `the_post_thumbnail()`), $width, $height, and $crop. $crop (which is false by default) tells WordPress if it should do a hard crop. A hard crop will crop to the exact dimensions specified, regardless of aspect ratio. If $crop is false, it will do a soft or proportional crop. The image's width and height are treated as maximum dimensions.

So when you upload an image, at least three new images (or different sizes) are created. Because of this, the file size is affected; smaller images will have smaller files sizes. We can take advantage of these images by calling them using a light-weight JavaScript library called picturefill.js to show the appropriately sized images based on screen size.

Using picturefill.js

picturefill.js was created by Scott Jehl to mimic functionality for a proposed `<picture>` HTML element that would nicely handle responsive (and even Retina-ready) images. All of the information about it can be found at http://rwdwp.com/23.

To use it, you list several lines in this format:

```
<span data-src="image.jpg" data-media="(min-width: 400px)"></span>
```

The `data-src` is the image source, and the `data-media` is the Media Query at which the image should be used. A full block might look like this example on GitHub:

```
<span data-picture data-alt="A giant stone face at The Bayon
temple in Angkor Thom, Cambodia">
<span data-src="small.jpg"></span>
<span data-src="medium.jpg"
→data-media="(min-width: 400px)"></span>
<span data-src="large.jpg"
→data-media="(min-width: 800px)"></span>
```

```
<span data-src="extralarge.jpg"
→data-media="(min-width: 1000px)"></span>

        <!-- Fallback content for non-JS browsers. Same img src
         →as the initial, unqualified source element. -->
<noscript>
<img src="external/imgs/small.jpg" alt="A giant stone face at
→The Bayon temple in Angkor Thom, Cambodia">
</noscript>
</span>
```

The first one is assumed to be for the smallest screens, and you can have as many entries/Media Queries as you like. The GitHub page talks about various uses before the basic example here, but this will serve us well.

As you might imagine, we can use this script along with the multiple image sizes produced by WordPress' Media Manager to automatically generate a picturefill object that can be called in your themes:

```
function mf_get_featured_image($html, $aid=false){
    $sizes= array('thumbnail', 'medium', 'large', 'full');

    $img= '<span data-picture data-alt="'.get_the_title().'">';
    $ct= 0;
    $aid= (!$aid) ? get_post_thumbnail_id() : $aid;

    foreach($sizes as $size){
        $url= wp_get_attachment_image_src($aid, $size);

        $width= ($ct < sizeof($sizes)-1) ? ($url[1]*0.66) :
        →($width/0.66)+25;

        $img.= '
            <span data-src="'. $url[0] .'"';
        $img.= ($ct > 0) ? ' data-media="(min-width: '.
        →$width .'px)"></span>' :'></span>';

        $ct++;
    }
```

```
$url= wp_get_attachment_image_src( $aid, $sizes[1]);
$img.=  '<noscript>
            <img src="'.$url[0] .'" alt="'.
            →get_the_title().'">
        </noscript>
    </span>';
    return $img;
}
```

There are a few things going on here. The first is that the function has an array of all the default sizes in WordPress. If you have your own sizes defined, you will have to add them here. This is so the picturefill element is accurately populated. After some setup (defining the image sizes, opening the picturefill element, initializing a counter), it moves through the $sizes, printing an image entry for each size.

For each entry, wp_get_attachment_image_src() is called to grab the URL of the image based on the image's ID (which get_post_thumbnail_id() returns based on the post ID) and the size. wp_get_attachement_image_src() returns an array that includes the image, the width, the height, and whether or not it's cropped. The first time through the Loop, we don't need to specify a minimum width, since that image will be a default. That's where the counter comes in. For the rest of the iterations, the width is calculated using a simple formula and an assumption. Let's look at that line again:

```
$width= ($ct < sizeof($sizes)-1) ? ($url[1]*0.66) :
→($width/0.66)+25;
```

What's happening here in most cases is that we start showing the next image size up at 66% the width of the image; so if the image is 1000px, it will start being shown at 660px. However, if it is the last image in the array, the assumption is that this is the biggest image (the image at full width). There are some strange results returned in some cases with this image, so you can't rely on the width and height returned with the full width image. We simply take the previous image's width and add 25px to it.

The last thing this function does before returning the picturefill code is set a default image in case JavaScript is disabled. The medium image is the default.

Since this plugin requires picturefill, one more task needs to be performed, and that's to actually add picturefill.js to the rest of the JavaScript loaded on the site. Looking at the mf_scripts() we've used throughout the book, you'll notice that

the line wp_enqueue_script('picturefill', TEMPPATH.'/js/picturefill.
js', array()); has already been added.

If you'd rather continue to use the_post_thumbnail() instead of a new function,
or if you want this to apply to all features images/instances of the_post_
thumbnail(), you can easily do that by adding this filter to your functions.php file:

```
add_filter( 'post_thumbnail_html', 'mf_get_featured_image');
```

It's important to note that this function will not automatically run for all images
on pages and blog posts; this is strictly for getting featured post images. To
replace all post images would require content filters, as well as some regex magic
to replace the <img> tag with the picturefill script.

There is a plugin available that will replace content images with picturefill, located
at http://rwdwp.com/37. Based on my testing, it works fairly well, but you may see
performance issues. That said, this might be your best bet as what I was experi-
menting with returned worse performance than the plugin.

Moving forward, you can also use a shortcode, along with the above function.
I didn't touch on the arguments the function accepts, but the first is $html; this
is the HTML send by the post_thumbnail_html filter. The second is $aid, for
attachment ID. This will allow you to call the function on any image you want,
not just featured ones.

The shortcode you're going to create is [mf_image src='path/to/image']. This
is a shortcode that will accept a URL for an argument and print out the picturefill
markup for that image. The function that does the heavy lifting is a modified version of one by wpmu.org (http://rwdwp.com/38) and is listed below, but first let's
look at the function used for the actual shortcode:

```
function mf_responsive_image($atts, $content=null){
    extract( shortcode_atts( array(
        'src' => false
    ), $atts ) );

    if(!$src){
        return '';
    }else{
        $aid= mf_get_attachment_id_from_src($src);
        $img= mf_get_featured_image('', $aid);
    }
```

NOTE

To support
featured images,
you will need to
add add_theme_
support('post-
thumbnails');
to your functions.
php file.

```
    return $img;

}

add_shortcode('mf_image', 'mf_responsive_image');
```

The function will check to make sure a URL is passed, then grab the ID for that URL (that's where wpmu.org's function comes in) before passing that ID off to the `mf_get_featured_image` function. It will then return the HTML generated. Here is the function that grabs the attachment ID based on the URL:

```
function mf_get_attachment_id_from_src($url) {
    global $wpdb;
    $prefix = $wpdb->prefix;
    $attachment = $wpdb->get_col($wpdb->prepare("SELECT ID
        ⇥FROM " . $prefix . "posts" . " WHERE guid='%s';", $url ));
    return $attachment[0];
}
```

Between the shortcode and the featured image function, you have two good methods for using picturefill and responsive images moving forward. Hopefully an efficient way to do all images will emerge in the near future. In the meantime, there is another method that can be used to make images a bit more responsive-friendly.

Overriding Set Width and Height

This is a technique that Jesse Friedman put forth in his book, *Web Designer's Guide to WordPress*. jQuery would allow us to search for all `<img>` tags in the content and remove the set width and height attributes applied to images. This will, at the very least, ensure that the images resize properly:

```
$(function(){
    $(".post img").removeAttr("width").removeAttribute("height");
}
```

You can add this function to your header (or even better, using add_action) and enqueue jQuery, and you're all set.

CSS may also be used for the technique, though results may vary based on custom posts, images, and other CSS rules; because of that, this code may need to be tweaked:

```
img[class*="align"],
img[class*="wp-image-"] {
  height: auto; }

img.size-full {
  width: auto; }
```

Handling Widgets

Sidebars and widgets are a staple of many sites, including those powered by WordPress. The WordPress admin makes it incredibly easy for end users to manage their own sidebars; however, it's up to you to ensure that the sidebars and widgets don't break when it comes to responsive design. First, let's look at responsive sidebars.

The Sidebar

It's worth noting right off the bat that using the term *sidebar* (at least in this book) doesn't necessarily mean the physical location of this content. The sidebar can be any auxiliary content. It just so happens that the main example of our sidebar is on the right side.

Responsive sidebar development starts right at the beginning of the coding process, in determining where in the markup the sidebar will go. It's important to structure and stack each column properly, especially when taking a Mobile First approach to development; if we don't, it might be the case that on small screens, the sidebar shows first, and then the main content area.

The way content should be structured or stacked is Header > Main Content > Sidebars > Footer (**Figure 4.10**).

TIP
Proper page structure also helps with search engine optimization. By placing the main content first, it tells search engines, "This is more important."

Figure 4.10
Here is the Content stack, illustrated for a three-column layout.

The Millennium Flights site actually only has a right sidebar, so the structure of things in the HTML will look like this:

```
<div id="content" class="group">
    <div class="entry">
        <!--Content Goes Here-->
    </div>
    <aside class="sidebar">
        <!--Widgets Go Here-->
    </aside>
</div>
```

Notice that the div with the id "content" serves as a container for both the main content area and the sidebar. The div "entry" will be for the site's main content, and the aside element will house the sidebar.

Since the sections are in the proper order, there is actually no CSS required for smaller screens, layout wise. Any pre–Media Query styles will be strictly for some padding, font adjustments, image aligning, and so on. However, once the screen reaches a certain width, it's time to move the entire sidebar up to the right, next to the main content area. The CSS looks like this:

```
@media screen and (min-width: 40.625em){
    #wrapper #content .entry{
        float: left;
        width: 66%;
    }

    #wrapper #content aside{
        margin-left: 68%;
        width: 30%;
    }
}
```

If you've worked with non-fluid (or fixed) layouts, this should look familiar to you. The main content area, .entry, is being floated to the left and limited to a width of 66%. The sidebar is then given a slightly larger margin and a width that accounts for the extra spacing. As users expand out even more, we may want the sidebar and content area to adjust further so the content and sidebar look proportionally better compared to the width of the screen:

```
@media screen and (min-width: 55.652em){
    #wrapper #content .entry{
        float: left;
        width: 75%;
        }

    #wrapper #content aside{
        margin-left: 78%;
        width: 22%;
        }
}
```

As you develop, it's important to test and try different layouts along the way. Remember—the breakpoints are based on content, not device! Do what's best for your own content.

That's all we need as far as structural CSS goes for the sidebar. Of course, now there is the question of handling widgets…

The .group Class

In order to ensure there is no runaway floating content without using the common .clearfix class, the .group class can be used. This technique was put forth by Dan Cederholm as a better alternative that cuts down on markup. The CSS looks like this:

```
.group:after {
    content: ".";
    display: block;
    height: 0;
    clear: both;
    visibility: hidden;
    }
```

This will make the containing class "self-clearing" and alleviate the need for an empty container. It's worth noting that the :after pseudo-class does not work in IE7 and below.

Sidebar Widgets

A widget in WordPress is defined as adding features and content to sidebars. Generally speaking, they are boxes placed outside the main content area that can contain any kind of content—text, images, forms, and so on. As designers and developers, we should plan to support these elements and more, as there are hundreds (perhaps thousands) of widgets out there.

TIP
When developing your own plugins or widgets for release, use the least amount of CSS possible and make it easily available to theme editors who might want to change it.

First, you must properly register your sidebars to use containers and class names you assign. Here's what's added in the Millennium Flights theme:

```
register_sidebar( array (
    'name' => __( 'Sidebar', 'main-sidebar' ),
    'id' => 'primary-widget-area',
    'description' => __( 'The primary widget area', 'wpbp' ),
    'before_widget' => '<div class="widget">',
    'after_widget' => "</div>",
    'before_title' => '<h3 class="widget-title">',
    'after_title' => '</h3>',
) );

register_sidebar( array (
    'name' => __( 'Sidebar2', 'secondary-sidebar' ),
    'id' => 'secondary-widget-area',
    'description' => __( 'The secondary widget area', 'wpbp' ),
    'before_widget' => '<div class="widget">',
    'after_widget' => "</div>",
    'before_title' => '<h3 class="widget-title">',
    'after_title' => '</h3>',
) );
```

You can see that the same structure is used for both sidebars. Each widget gets the class "widget," and the titles are <h3> tags with the class "widget-title." This will allow you to apply general styles to HTML elements without them being overridden by other plugins.

In the Millennium Flights theme, before any Media Queries, there are some basic styles applied to elements you might find in a sidebar widget. These will also optimize certain elements (like form fields) for touchscreen devices.

```css
aside .widget h3{
    margin-top: 0px;
    color: #8E6DD7;
    }

aside .widget{
    border-bottom: 2px solid #FFFFFF;
    margin: 10px 1.5%;
    text-align: left;
    padding: 5px 0.4%;
    }

aside .widget p, aside .widget ul,
aside .widget ol, aside .widget dl{
    margin: 0;
    padding: 0;
    font-size: 1.2em;
    }

aside .widget li{
    padding: 0;
    margin: 0 0 0 1em;
    list-style-type: none;
    }

aside .widget input, aside .widget select{
    margin: 1%;
    padding: 7px;
    font-size: 1.6em;
    width: 100%;
    border: 1px solid #CFCFCF;
    -moz-border-radius: 10px;
    -webkit-border-radius: 10px;
    -o-border-radius: 10px;
    border-radius: 10px;
    }
```

Then, as users move to larger screens, only slight adjustments are needed:

```
@media screen and (min-width: 40.625em){
aside .widget input[type=submit], aside .widget
input[type=button]{
        margin: 0 auto;
        padding: 3px;
        font-size: 1.25em;
        width: 40%;
        }

    footer aside .widget{
        width: 30%;
        margin: 10px 1.2%;
        float: left;
        text-align: left;
        }
    }
```

As a matter of fact, very little needs to be done here. There is a small adjustment for submits and buttons, and some styles for the widgets found in the footer, which should be placed three per line. However, there is a small issue with this approach.

I ran into a situation where a breakpoint was already added to a previous layout I was using, so I kept it in. If you look at the page with a screen width of 40em (650px), the widgets are a bit scrunched (**Figure 4.11**).

Figure 4.11
The footer widgets at 650px are a bit too scrunched to be three per line.

Because of this, I needed to determine new breakpoints. Here's what the new adjustments look like in the CSS:

```css
@media screen and (min-width: 34.188em){
    ...
    footer aside .widget{
        width: 46%;
        margin: 10px 1.2%;
        float: left;
        text-align: left;
        }
}
@media screen and (min-width: 51em){
    footer aside .widget{
        width: 30%;
        }
}
```

I created two new breakpoints—one for a two-column widget layout and one for a three-column layout. Things look much better with the 3-column layout now (**Figure 4.12**).

Figure 4.12 With the adjusted breakpoints, the widgets look much better.

As you continue to add widgets to your theme, it's important to consider the following:

◆ Is the widget properly coded? Will it use the HTML structure you defined when registering the sidebars?

◆ Does it come with its own complicated CSS? If it does, overriding styles (especially if they are inline) might be a pain in the neck due to the need to nest classes and be incredibly specific with your style selectors.

◆ Does the author make the class names intuitive and easy to find (through documentation)? If so, you'll have an easier time styling for them.

If you properly plan and code consistently, you shouldn't run into issues with your widgets. Between the reset, default element styles, and default widget styles discussed in this chapter, most bases should be covered.

Wrapping Up

We explored quite a bit in this chapter, from several navigation techniques using Media Queries, RESS, and JavaScript to making our images respond to both screen resolutions and connection speeds, as well as making the most out of our sidebar widgets.

Images proved to be a tough task to tackle, but we can now replace featured images automatically and post images with a shortcode. While images still remain a bit of a question mark as far as the best way to replace in-content images on a large scale due to some possible performance issues, what we looked at will at least help you and your users moving forward. Trying to fix all images at load time puts a lot of stress on the website that results in it being visibly slower. Hopefully we will see this improved upon in the near future.

Since this chapter focused primarily on layout elements, in the next chapter we will go back to WordPress' roots and look at making elements of the blog portion of a site responsive. Specifically, we'll look at comments, archives, and other developers' plugins.

Questions

1. What is the biggest pitfall of the "Do Nothing" navigation approach?

2. When should RESS be employed in regard to navigation?

3. What does picturefill.js do?

4. How do you ensure content integrity as far as multicolumn layouts are concerned?

Answers

1. It will take up a lot of vertical space, pushing the content down the page.

2. RESS should be employed when we are hiding navigation/markup based on screen width.

3. It replaces a single `<img>` with multiple image options, to be displayed based on screen width.

4. Structure the columns so the main content is on top, followed by the sidebars.

Chapter 5

Making Your Theme Responsive: Blog Features

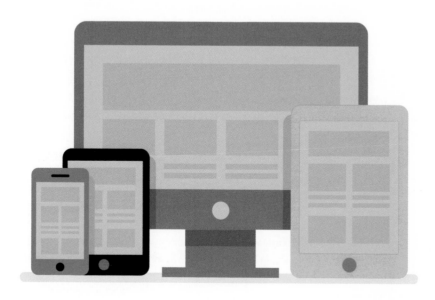

Now that we've looked at some of the core features of WordPress (and really, a lot of websites), we have a few solid methods for handling layouts and the most bandwidth-heavy content. Chapter 4 was called "Making Your Theme Responsive: Core Features" because what we covered is built into the fabric of every website in one way or another. We just put the WordPress spin on it. But there are a few features that are uniquely WordPress.

WordPress started as a blogging platform long ago, and, for many, it is still just that. Even if you are using it for more (and recent statistics say that's most of you), the blog portion of WordPress is still very much alive and well. Even if a site isn't a blog, it probably still has a blog, or a news section, or announcements. Blogs are part of the very fabric of WordPress, which is why it's important to explore the best ways to take "blog features" and adapt them to a responsive design.

We won't necessarily look at things like dates and other post metadata since that's all handled with CSS, but we will address both comments and archives (including search), as well as plugins. While plugins aren't necessarily blog-specific, they have been with WordPress from very early on; also, where navigation, images, and sidebars can be used on other sites, WordPress plugins are distinctive.

Handling Comments

TIP

Don't feed the trolls.

Comments are the pulse of a blog—they welcome discussion, start debates, and can even be a breeding ground for trolls. They are a great supplement for content; however, a lot of comments can really increase the loading time and the length of the page. A quick and easy fix would be to hide the comments on mobile, but we know well enough by now the reasons not to do this.

Instead we'll look at two different techniques designed to not only display comments that look nice on smaller screens, but improve performance of the website and overall UX.

Styling the Comments Section

No matter what solution you decide to go with, there will always be the issue of styling the comments in an easy-to-read way; there are countless ways to do this, of course. In this section, we will take advantage of the groundwork that we laid earlier in the book. There are two parts to styling the comments section: the comments themselves, and the comment form.

Commenting Systems

Aside from WordPress' built-in commenting system, there are several other popular methods for managing comments used by websites, including WordPress. There are several advantages to using these third-party systems, including the fact that sections are customizable but for the most part already styled for you, and they handle authentication and moderation from a dashboard completely separate from WordPress.

One popular method is Disqus (http://rwdwp.com/39), which allows users to place comments on any webpage using JavaScript. It allows users to manage multiple comment areas across several sites and lets commenters log in using one of many social media login credentials, including Facebook and Twitter. There is even a WordPress plugin: http://rwdwp.com/40.

A second very popular method is using Facebook-embedded comments. Then any user logged in to Facebook will be able to comment, and even get response notifications from Facebook itself. There are a few plugins and tutorials out there to help you, but nothing official for WordPress integration.

Deciding which commenting system to use comes down to several factors, including ownership. One question you should ask yourself is if the service goes away or you want to move off of it, will you be able to get those comments via export or backup?

STYLING THE COMMENTS

When styling the comments, there are a few pieces of information that need to be considered: name, URL, date and time, the user's avatar, and the comment itself. WordPress generates the comments using an ordered list, where each comment is a list item; this gives developers the option of numbering the comments.

Aside from information that should be displayed, you also need to take into account nested comments and admin, editor, and author comments. Both of these can be styled as normal comments, but if you want them to stand out, you'll have to add in some extra CSS.

Let's start with some initial styles:

```
ol.commentlist{
    margin-left: 0;
    padding-left: 0;
    }

ol.commentlist li{
    padding: 1em;
```

NOTE

WordPress uses its own service, Gravatar (http://rwdwp.com/41) for commenters' photos. By default, if a user wants a photo displayed, he will have to get a Gravatar account, otherwise a generic photo will display. There is, however, a plugin that allows you to use local (non-Gravatar) images: http://rwdwp.com/42.

```
        list-style-type: none;
        border-bottom: 2px solid #FFFFFF;
        }

    ol.commentlist li .vcard img{
        float: left;
        padding-right: 0.4em;
        }
```

The styles above will give you the results shown in **Figure 5.1**.

Next is to add some styles to make author comments stick out and comment replies display nicely on smaller screens:

```
    ol.commentlist li.bypostauthor{
        background: #FFFFFF;
        color: #313C66;
        }

    ol.commentlist li.bypostauthor a{
        color: #624A14;
        }

    ol.commentlist li ul{
        margin: 0;
        padding: 0;
        }

    ol.commentlist li li{
        border-bottom: 0;
        border-left: 3px solid #77A4AE;
        font-size: 1em;
        }
```

WordPress automatically applies a.bypostauthor class to author comments, which makes it very easy to style and set apart. Here, you are changing the background and text color just to set those comments apart from the other comments.

Figure 5.1 Here is what the comments with some basic CSS applied will look like on mobile.

Figure 5.2 The comments section on a wide screen, showing both author comments and indented replies.

For replies, WordPress uses an unordered list (`<ul>`), so the first task is to remove any padding or margins from that. As the screen gets wider, replies will be indented, but to save screen space on smaller screens, they will not yet. Instead, you are using a 3px border on the left to denote a reply.

Speaking of expanding outward, there isn't too much to do regarding that. You will set a max-width on the comment boxes, add some indentation to replies, and that's about it.

```
@media screen and (min-width: 51em){
    ...
    ol.commentlist{
        max-width: 70%;
        }

    ol.commentlist li ul{
        margin-left: 2em;
        }
}
```

These are just a couple of simple styles that improve the layout once the user's screen hits 51em. Here is the final, widescreen result (**Figure 5.2**).

STYLING THE COMMENT FORM

Possibly more important than making it easy for users to read comments is making it easy for them to submit comments. Here's what the comment form looks like without doing any extra work (**Figure 5.3**).

Figure 5.3
The unstyled comment form makes input pretty difficult.

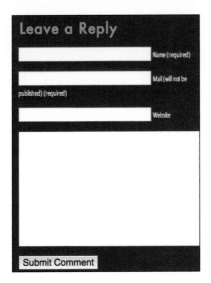

Luckily, you can solve this with just a few lines of CSS:

```
form#commentform input, form#commentform textarea{
    margin: 0.4em;
    padding: 0.5em;
    font-size: 1.3em;
    border: 1px solid #CFCFCF;
    -moz-border-radius: 10px;
    -webkit-border-radius: 10px;
    -o-border-radius: 10px;
    border-radius: 10px;
    }

form#commentform textarea{
    max-height: 150px;
    max-width: 95%;
    }
```

```
form#commentform label{
    font-size: 1.25em;
    }
```

This will essentially do the same thing that you did with the search form element, increasing the size of the box and text and making the form easier to read and use. As the screen gets wider, thanks to some default styles that were added to the theme earlier and how WordPress prints out the elements, you don't actually need to do anything to make the form look nice (**Figure 5.4**).

Now that the CSS is taken care of, let's look at three things that will help loading times and overall UX: pagination, incremental loading, and a separate comments page.

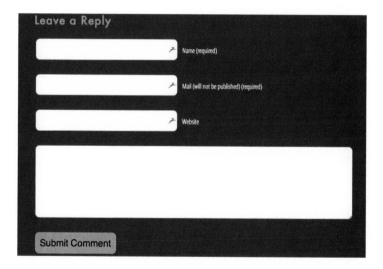

Figure 5.4 The full-width form without any additional CSS. Because of default styles already in the CSS, the form doesn't need any modification to work properly.

Customizing the Comments Form

If you decide you'd really like to customize the layout of the form on top of the styles, there are several ways to do so. The function that calls the comments form, aptly named `comment_form()`, accepts several arguments, including a `$fields` argument that allows you to replace the fields already there with your own. You can see an example on the function's Codex page: http://rwdwp.com/43.

You can also add or remove fields from your form using the `comment_form_default_fields` filter, which will use a callback function you write to modify the `$fields` array. There is a fantastic tutorial on how to do all of that and more at http://rwdwp.com/44.

Pagination

This technique is the easiest to implement because it is essentially changing a setting in the WordPress admin. You can choose how many comments to show per page, if you want to do nesting, as well as other customizations (**Figure 5.5**).

Figure 5.5
The WordPress admin area has some built-in functionality for limiting the number of comments shown on a page.

As far as implementing pagination, there's not much more you have to do than include a single template tag—the same one used to include comments and the comment form:

```php
<?php comments_template(); ?>
```

This technique allows you to get the comments up and running quickly, but there is one big drawback: moving to the next set of comments means the entire page needs to be loaded again. This is OK if the user doesn't want to read all of the comments; only the first set of comments is loaded and that's that. But if the user wants to read more, she is out of luck.

Incremental Loading

The biggest issue with comments is that they don't scale well. As more comments are added, the length of the page grows, and the size of the page with it. Paginating helps this a little. You're setting the number of comments to a finite amount per page. If we are able to implement pagination without reloading the page to view new comments, we can cut down on initial load time, save the users bandwidth, and then load comments only if the user wants to read them.

There is a WordPress plugin that will load a page first, and then the comments later; it's called AJAX Comment Loading and can be found at http://rwdwp. com/45. This would likely do well in a lot of cases, and will load the primary content faster. However, this wouldn't solve the other problems of page length and saving on bandwidth. For that, some coding is required.

First, you are going to need to modify the comments display in your theme—
specifically, you will be adding one class to the navigation: #commentsNav. This
will require you to create a new template in your theme called comments.php.
Here is the code in its entirety:

```php
<?php
// Do not delete these lines
if (!empty($_SERVER['SCRIPT_FILENAME']) && 'comments.php' ==
→basename($_SERVER['SCRIPT_FILENAME']))
    die ('Please do not load this page directly. Thanks!');
if ( post_password_required() ) { ?>
    <p class="nocomments">This post is password protected.
    →Enter the password to view comments.</p>
<?php
    return;
}
?>
<!-- You can start editing here. -->

<?php if ( have_comments() ) : ?>
    <h3 id="comments"><?php comments_number('No Comments',
    →'One Comment', '% Comments' );?> to &#8220;<?php
    →the_title(); ?>&#8221;</h3>

    <ol class="commentlist">
    <?php wp_list_comments(); ?>
    </ol>

    <div id="commentNav" class="navigation group">
        <div class="alignleft"><?php previous_comments_link() ?>
        →</div>
        <div class="alignright"><?php next_comments_link() ?>
        →</div>
    </div>
<?php else : // this is displayed if there are no comments so
→far ?>
    <?php if ( comments_open() ) : ?>
        <!-- If comments are open, but there are no comments. -->
```

```php
<?php else : // comments are closed ?>
    <!-- If comments are closed. -->
    <p class="nocomments">Comments are closed.</p>
<?php endif; ?>
<?php endif; ?>
<?php if ( comments_open() ) : ?>
<?php comment_form(); ?>
<?php endif; // if you delete this the sky will fall on your
→head ?>
```

TIP

A way to bypass hooks, filters, and functions but still modify the comment form is to replace the comment_form() call in comments. php with your own code. Proceed with caution, though; it's kind of hacky to do it that way.

The inline comments should help here, but here's essentially what's happening:

1. You are disabling direct access to this file.

2. You are printing the comments and navigation.

3. You are printing the form.

The next (and final) step is to add a bit of jQuery to single pages to turn the comment navigation links into AJAX calls instead of hyperlinks:

```php
function mf_ajax_comments(){
    if(is_single()){
        echo '<script type="text/javascript" charset="utf-8">
            jQuery(document).ready(function(){
                jQuery(\'#commentNav a\').
                →live(\'click\', function(e){
                    e.preventDefault();
                    var link = jQuery(this).attr(\'href\');
                    jQuery(\'#commentsection\').
                    →html(\'Loading...\');
                    jQuery(\'#commentsection\').
                    →load(link+\' #commentsection\');
                });
            });
        </script>';
    }
}

add_action('wp_head', 'mf_ajax_comments');
```

What this is doing is (if the page is a single post) printing jQuery code that will take the hyperlink, grab it from the server, and place the content in the specified div. Remember to enqueue jQuery in your theme if you haven't already. The best part is that this is relatively lightweight and will save the user from having to reload a full page each time.

A Separate Comments Page

If you want to give users access to the comments without loading them at all on the post's page, you could create a separate page with just comments on them.

While WordPress doesn't support this natively, there are luckily tools out there to get single comment pages working. There is a plugin out on GitHub called wp-comments-page: http://rwdwp.com/46. Download that and upload storm-comments-page.php to plugins/. Then upload comments-single.php to your theme directory.

Three things need to happen to make this plugin function properly. First, enable it from the WordPress admin area. Then, you will need to add some code to your theme. Create a template in your theme named comments-single.php (uploading the page that came with the plugin is fine, though you may need to customize it). The way the plugin works is it will register this template name with WordPress, allowing it to access the current query, which is based on the URL (more on that in a bit). This is the code that should go in the template file:

```php
<?php get_header(); ?>
<div class="entry">
        <h2>Comments for <a href="<?php the_permalink(); ?>">
        →<?php the_title(); ?></a></h2>
        <div id="commentsection">
            <ol class="commentlist">
            <?php
                wp_list_comments('reverse_top_level=false',
                →get_comments('post_id='.$post->ID));
            comment_form();
            ?>
            </ol>
        </div>
</div>
<?php get_footer(); ?>
```

You should notice a couple of things going on here; first, you have the `.commentsection` class, and more importantly, you're wrapping the WordPress code in `<ol class="commentslist">` tags. This is because `wp_list_comments()` does not include the outer wrapper that `comments_template()` includes, so in order to make sure the comments are styled properly, you must add the `<ol>` wrapper.

Now you have a template tag capable of displaying a separate comments page. There are a couple of caveats, though. The first is that you will have to manually link to this page since `comments_popup_link()` does not have any hooks/ filters. This can be as simple as changing `<?php comments_popup_link(); ?>` to `<a href="<?php the_permalink(); ?>comments/">Comments</a>` in the single. php template. This does bring up a second issue, however: permalinks need to be enabled for this to work. The plugin registers a rewrite function to call the comments-single.php template with the correct permalink structure. Any permalink structure should do.

Finally, this method does not handle comment pagination (at the time of this writing). Therefore, you will need to turn that off in the WordPress admin in order to display all of the comments. Here is the final result (**Figure 5.6**).

Figure 5.6 Here is the full-width version of the comments-only page. Because it uses the same styles as the single blog post page, we know it looks good on mobile too.

Adding the Comment Count to the Single Page Link

One drawback of using this method is that you lose the comment count. Luckily WordPress has a built-in function called `comments_number()` (or `get_comment_number()` if you don't want to print it automatically), which will retrieve the number of comments in a format determined by the arguments you send. Instead of manually printing the permalink in the templates where you want to link to the comments, you can create a function that includes the comment count, like this:

```
function mf_comments_page_link(){
echo '<a href="'. get_permalink() . 'comments/">'.
→get_comments_number() .' Comments</a>';
}
```

You can then replace the static link with this function call.

Handling Archives

A blog's archives are important; they give users a way to access older (but hopefully still useful) content. It's a completely separate way of navigating through the website, and in some ways it's even more important to make sure this navigation is easy to use because archives can grow pretty quickly. Stepping away from Millennium Flights for a moment, here's a screenshot of an archives list from a blog that's been around for nearly 10 years (**Figure 5.7**).

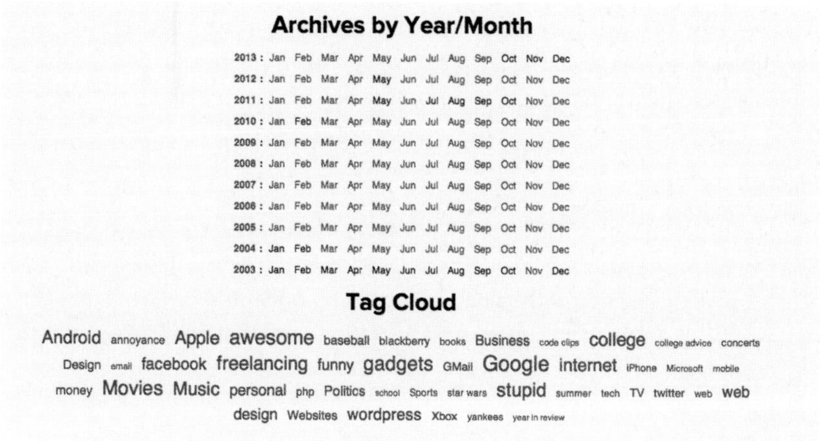

Figure 5.7
Casabona.org's blog (hey, that name sounds familiar!) has archives dating back 10 years; it's important that this archive is organized and easy to use.

In Figure 5.7, you'll see that there are two elements to the archive page: a block organized by year and month, and a tag cloud, which is simply a block of tags where the size of the tag is dependent on the number of posts associated with it. But this can be improved. There are several usability aspects to keep in mind, especially for mobile, when creating a good archives page.

Considerations to Make for a Better User Experience

One big way to improve the implementation shown in Figure 5.7 would be to add a search bar front and center for users to look for specific content instead of guessing by date or tag. Informally speaking, a lot of people I talk to mention they prefer to use a site's search function over anything else when looking for information. The size of the text for the year/month listing could also stand to be increased, especially when being viewed on a mobile device. Finally, listing categories as well as tags might be something visitors to the site would find useful.

Aside from a separate archives page, a common practice is to include archives by date and category lists in the sidebar. WordPress has built-in widgets to support both of these features. However, it's important to be mindful of how these will scale as more dates and categories are added.

In this section, we will actually look at implementations for all four of these elements: dates, categories, tags, and search. The main concerns will be mobile experience as well as ensuring that these implementations scale well.

Archives by Date

Archives by date have proven to be the most difficult to do well because they will keep growing as long as you have a blog that you keep updated. Archives are organized by year, month, and day, but generally listing by year and month will suffice.

A look at the built-in WordPress widget for Archives by Date can be found in **Figure 5.8**.

By default, the widget will list all of the archives (month, year) as an unordered list. As you can imagine, the longer the blog is active, the longer this list gets, taking up a large portion of the sidebar. Those who work on WordPress thought of this and now offer an alternate implementation—one that will list the archives as a drop-down menu instead of a long list. This is something we've seen before:

It was presented as a mobile alternative for website navigation. For a sidebar widget, this method works out quite nicely both in full-width views and on smaller screens, especially mobile devices (**Figure 5.9**).

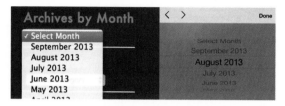

Figure 5.8 For reference, here is the Archives widget that comes built in to WordPress.

Figure 5.9 Archives by Date as a drop-down menu. On the left, full-width/desktop view. On the right, an iOS 7 device, which has a special implementation for using drop-down menus.

While this works for a sidebar, where the space is limited (width-wise and height-wise), doing a main content/page implementation should take a little more work; there should be a bigger focus on the archives when they are part of the main content area.

Looking back at Figure 5.7, the years and months are nicely laid out as rows and columns (though no tables are used), and users can easily see which months have posts and which months don't. The archives here are using a great plugin called Compact Archives (http://rwdwp.com/47) which will also be used in the following examples. The plugin does all of the heavy lifting regarding the logic for printing the archives in this way; it offers shortcodes, template tags, and multiple views, and it even allows you to choose the markup for before and after each element.

WORDPRESS ARCHIVE TEMPLATES

Before we get started in this section, I should note that there are two types of archives templates we're going to look at: the supported archive templates that are automatically generated by the WordPress template hierarchy, and a page template that is conventionally named archives.php.

WordPress supports potentially thousands of different archive templates, allowing anything from individual author pages (author-$id.php) or tag pages (tag-$slug.php) to a general category.php page. There is a single catch-all (besides index.php), which will be applied to any type of archive page in a specific template's absence: archive.php. The information on the archive.php template page is

TIP

A lot of web developers consider tables to be taboo. The thing is, tables are great—for tabular data. The case could be made for using a table for the compact archives.

generally very similar (if not identical) to the information displayed on the index.
php template. The main difference is that there is some logic to tell the user which
archive is being viewed:

```php
<?php if (have_posts()) : ?>
<?php $post = $posts[0]; // Hack. Set $post so that the_date()
→works. ?>
<?php /* If this is a category archive */ if (is_category())
→{ ?>
        <h2 class="pagetitle">Category: <?php
        →single_cat_title(); ?></h2>
<?php /* If this is a tag archive */ } elseif( is_tag() ) { ?>
<h2 class="pagetitle">Posts Tagged &#8216;<?php
→single_tag_title(); ?>&#8217;</h2>
<?php /* If this is a daily archive */ } elseif (is_day()) { ?>
        <h2 class="pagetitle"><?php the_time('F jS, Y'); ?>
        →Archive</h2>
<?php /* If this is a monthly archive */ } elseif (is_month())
→{ ?>
        <h2 class="pagetitle"><?php the_time('F, Y'); ?>
        →Archive</h2>
<?php /* If this is a yearly archive */ } elseif (is_year())
→{ ?>
        <h2 class="pagetitle"><?php the_time('Y'); ?>
        →Archive</h2>
<?php /* If this is an author archive */ } elseif (is_author())
→{ ?>
<h2 class="pagetitle">Author Archive</h2>
<?php /* If this is a paged archive */ } elseif
→(isset($_GET['paged']) && !empty($_GET['paged'])) { ?>
        <h2 class="pagetitle">Blog Archives</h2>
<?php } ?>
```

This code is essentially checking the WordPress query to see what kinds of posts
were returned and how they were organized. It then displays the title accordingly.

These pages actually have nothing to do with the page you are creating in this
section. These are simply another way to display posts. You will be creating the
archives.php page, which, strictly speaking, is not a recognized template in the

The WordPress URL Query

WordPress is powered by a lot of sophisticated programming; part of that programming comes in parsing permalinks, looking for clues as to which data it's going to populate the page with.

What it does is convert a URL (say, millenniumflights.com/2013/12/hello-world) to a query string based on the permalinks structure chosen in the WordPress admin. In this case, it will grab "hello-world," which it has stored as the %postname% (notation same as on the Settings->Permalinks page). It will check to see what post ID corresponds with that post name and create a query string. So if the post's ID is 1, the query string WordPress uses might look like this, including the built-in query function: `query_posts('p=1')`.

This will work for any content called in WordPress.

WordPress hierarchy. This is simply a page template (like page-home.php). It will start off like this:

```php
<?php
/*
Template Name: Archives
*/
?>


<?php get_header(); ?>
```

It will also end with the regular `<?php get_footer(); ?>` tag. It's in the middle that you add things like a tag cloud or the Compact Archives. To activate this page, treat it like any other page template: Create a new page in the WordPress admin, give it a title, and then select "Archives" from the page template list on the right.

It's now time to explore creating the Compact Archives section of the archives. php page. Once the plugin is installed and activated, add this to the archives.php, under the `get_header()` call:

```html
<div class="post">

<h2>Archives</h2>
<ul class="compact-archives">
    <?php compact_archive('block'); ?>
</ul>
```

This will create a simple unordered list with the following markup:

```
<ul class="compact-archives">
    <li><strong><a href=$yearLink>$year</a>:</strong>
    →<a href="$janLink">Jan</a> <a href="$febLink">Feb</a> ...
    →<a href="$decLink">Dec</a></li>
    ...
</ul>
```

Any month without posts will be wrapped like this: `<span class="emptymonth">` `Mon</span>`. With this in mind, here are some mobile-friendly styles to place before any breakpoints are defined, in style.css:

```css
ul.compact-archives{
    margin: 0.7em;
    padding: 0;
    }

ul.compact-archives li{
    list-style-type: none;
    line-height: 2em;
    margin: 0.6em;
    }

ul.compact-archives li strong{
    font-weight: bold;
    display: block;
    border-bottom: 1px solid #999999;
    }

ul.compact-archives li a, ul.compact-archives li span{
    font-size: 1.7em;
    padding: 0 0.2em;
    }

ul.compact-archives li span.emptymonth{
    color: #CFCFCF;
    }
```

This will apply appropriate padding and font sizes to make the months easy to press with a finger. It will also gray out any months without posts. Finally, `display: block` is being applied to the year, which is wrapped in a `<strong>` tag. This allows you to treat the year as a header, clearly separating each year into sections and making it easy for users to quickly glance at. The resulting page looks something like what you see in **Figure 5.10**.

Figure 5.10 The Archive by Date section for Millennium Flights. The years are easy to differentiate, and the months are easy to select.

Expanding out and making the screen wider, you will want to make some adjustments to the CSS to make the archives nice and compact, as they were intended:

```
@media screen and (min-width: 34.188em){
    ul.compact-archives li strong{
        display: inline;
        border: 0;
        }

    ul.compact-archives li a, ul.compact-archives li span{
        font-size: 1.5em;
        }
}
```

With these adjustments, the year and months move to one line, and the text isn't as big. There is one more adjustment to make with wider screens, but we will save that for the tag cloud section.

Another way to save space without the use of CSS is to use RESS to conditionally view more compact views. The plugin offers two other views: "initial," which just displays the first letter of each month, and "numeric," which displays the number of each month. So in the archives.php template, you can have:

```php
<?php
    $view= (ISMOBILE) ? 'initial' : 'block';
    compact_archive($view);
?>
```

Using the `ISMOBILE` constant from the functions.php file, we can detect if users are on a small-screen device and display an even more compact version of the archives.

Working with Tag Clouds

Tag clouds are a lot of fun to work with and look at, and WordPress makes it very easy to create one; just a simple call to the built-in function `wp_tag_cloud()` with a few arguments for min and max size, and the units (px, em, %):

```php
<h2>Tag Cloud</h2>
<div class="tags">
    <?php wp_tag_cloud('smallest=0.9&largest=2.2&unit=em'); ?>
</div>
```

This will do the trick, and, honestly, it doesn't look too bad on smaller screens either (**Figure 5.11**).

Figure 5.11
The wide-screen view of the current tag cloud with the small-screen view embedded to the right.

There are optimizations that can be made for smaller screens so, for instance, users don't need to zoom in to select tags with lower counts. A fix for that might be to apply some default styles to the .tags div. Since ems are being used to represent font size, you can easily increase the font size by adding a rule like this:

```css
.tags{
    font-size: 2em;
    }
```

Then all the font sizes will automatically double. However, you may need to add styles later to override the font size as the screen gets larger. A nice implementation for smaller screens would be a long list of tags with a bar indicator of how many posts there are. To accomplish this, the first thing you need to do is replace the wp_tag_cloud() function. While this is a great function to generate a tag cloud, it doesn't provide a lot of flexibility. Instead, the following function, which uses get_terms(), will be used:

```php
function mf_tag_cloud($args=''){
    $tags = get_tags($args);
    $html = '<ul class="wp-tag-cloud">';
    foreach ( $tags as $tag ) {
        $tag_link = get_tag_link( $tag->term_id );
        $progress= $tag->count*2;
        $html .= "<li><a href='{$tag_link}'
        →title='{$tag->count} posts' class=
        →'{$tag->slug}'>{$tag->name}</a>";
        $html .= "<progress max='100' value='{$progress}'>
        →Count: {$tag->count}</progress></li>";
    }
    $html .= '</ul>';
    echo $html;
}
```

This function accepts a query string of arguments in the same fashion that get_tags() accepts it, and that is passed directly to get_tags(). With the returned tags, an unordered list of <progress> elements is generated, applying the number of posts for each tag as the "progress." That count is multiplied by two in this case to give the bars a little beefier look. Next it's time to apply the CSS:

```
ul.wp-tag-cloud{
    margin: 0;
    padding: 0.3em;
    }

ul.wp-tag-cloud li{
    list-style-type: none;
    }

ul.wp-tag-cloud li a{
    display: block;
    padding: 0.4em;
    margin: 0.3em 0;
    position: absolute;
    }

progress, progress[role] {
-moz-appearance: none;
    -webkit-appearance: none;
    appearance: none;
    border: none;
    background: #FFFFFF;
    background-size: auto;
    width: 100%;
    height: 4em;
    }

progress::-webkit-progress-bar {
    background: #FFFFFF;
    }

progress::-moz-progress-bar {
    background: #00FFFF;
    }

progress::-webkit-progress-value {
    background: #00FFFF;
    }
```

With the CSS, you are applying styles (including browser-specific ones) to the progress bar being displayed. Notice that the `<a>` elements are also positioned absolutely to make them appear as if they are inside the progress bar. The final step is to replace the code on archives.php:

```
<div class="tags">
<?php
        $args= "orderby=count&order=DESC&number=30";
        mf_tag_cloud($args);
?>
</div>
```

This generates a nice (bright!) progress bar that illustrates to users the most popular tags (**Figure 5.12**).

Figure 5.12
The Progress Bar UI as viewed on an iPhone using iOS 7.

Since this is a completely different implementation from the tag cloud, and one we want only on mobile devices, the best way to switch between the two is to use the `ISMOBILE` variable declared by the theme's RESS function. The final tag cloud code looks like this:

```
<div class="tags">
<?php
        if(ISMOBILE){
            $args= "orderby=count&order=DESC&number=30";
            mf_tag_cloud($args);
        }else{
```

```
            wp_tag_cloud('smallest=0.9&largest=2.2&unit=em');
        }
    ?>
</div>
```

NOTE
WordPress also has
a built-in Tag Cloud
widget.

Once the tag cloud is looking like a cloud again, there is one more thing you should do, going back to the reference made earlier with the Archives by Date section. Once the page gets wide enough, it would make sense to line up the two sections next to each other. This will take some minimal CSS, but you will have to add some extra markup to the archives.php template file. The tag cloud code is included for reference:

```
<div class="date-archives">
    <h2>Archives</h2>
    <ul class="compact-archives">
        <?php compact_archive('block'); ?>
    </ul>
</div>

<div class="tag-archives">
    <h2>Tag Cloud</h2>
    <div class="tags">
        <?php
            if(ISMOBILE){
                $args= "orderby=count&order=DESC&number=30";
                mf_tag_cloud($args);
            }else{
                wp_tag_cloud('smallest=0.9&largest=2.2&unit=em');
            }
        ?>
    </div>
</div>
```

Notice that there are two additional containers: .date-archives and .tag-archives. These will allow you to align the two sections side by side:

```
.date-archives{
    width: 58%;
    float: left;
```

```
        margin: 0 0.6em 0 0;
        }

  .tag-archives{
        width: 39%;
        float: right;
        margin: 0 0 0 0.6em;
        }
```

Before we look at the final product, there is one more element we need to take care of. But first…

USING CATEGORIES

Listing categories is a bit easier because generally there are fewer categories than tags. We won't explore thorough examples of various techniques, but you can imagine it's like displaying any sort of list of elements: Ensure that they are easy to select on smaller screens, and, as the user expands out, make sure he takes advantage of more space.

Much like the Date Archive widget in WordPress, there is also a Categories widget that will allow you to display the list of categories or a drop-down menu of items. This may be something you want to utilize on this archives page. It might also be worth it just to print the categories side-by-side like the compact archives for date.

Categories vs. Tags

Why are there fewer categories than tags? This might be something you know pretty well but need to articulate to clients and other WordPress users; it's also something important to keep in mind when developing Custom Post Types.

The main difference between the two is that categories organize posts by topic and tags serve as keywords that describe the post. So if the blog post was about space travel, the category might be "Recreation" and tags might be "space, travel, vacation, intergalactic, stellar."

The Search Bar

Even though the website has great implementations for both date-based and tag-based archives, it's highly likely that website visitors will still go for search when they can. That's why it's important to make this easily accessible from the archives page. At the top of your archives.php template, after the .post div, add this:

```
<h2>Search</h2>
<?php get_search_form(); ?>
```

This will add the search bar on top of everything else. With the general form styles, the input box and submit button look good, but there is a label that doesn't do much else besides take up space. You can remove that by creating your own searchform.php template; this will be used anywhere get_search_form() is used, including in the Search widget. Here is the full file:

```
<form role="search" method="get" id="searchform"
➔action="<?php echo home_url( '/' ); ?>">
<div>
<input type="text" value="" name="s" id="s"
➔placeholder="Search for..." />
<input type="submit" id="searchsubmit" value="Search" />
</div>
</form>
```

By replacing the label with a "placeholder" attribute, you can save a lot of space while also making the user aware of the input box's use. By placing this style rule under the 34.188em breakpoint, you will have a nice-looking, easy-to-use form for your users:

```
#searchform input[type=text]{
    width: 60%;
    }
```

MAKING SEARCH A LITTLE BETTER

There is one more way we can make search a little better. Typing can be cumbersome on a smaller device, especially when the user has to do a lot of it. One helpful improvement would be to add autocomplete for users, and luckily there are a couple of plugins that do that.

Before choosing to implement this, you should ask yourself if autocomplete is worth it. There is a jQuery plugin that is used for generating the terms and performing the autocompletion. Do the benefits of this plugin outweigh the fact that the user will have to download more JavaScript? How many jQuery plugins are too many? In this case, I would argue that that added script is beneficial because it doesn't weigh that much and it greatly improves UX. Most users have loaded jQuery somewhere along the way, so properly calling jQuery means the user has it cached already; it's really just a matter of downloading a small bit of code. Plus, jQuery 1.10 has made great strides in optimization. However, each case is different.

The two most popular plugins are SearchAutocomplete (http://rwdwp.com/48) and Autocompleter, though that is two years old. If you want to try your hand and code your own, WPTuts+ has a great tutorial: http://rwdwp.com/49.

WHAT ABOUT SEARCH RESULTS?

It's been a longstanding sentiment in the WordPress community that the built-in WordPress search is completely lacking (some have even said, "it sucks"). As of WordPress 3.7, which came out while this book was being written, search has been greatly improved. In that release, it does a much better job of combining keywords and ordering search results. WooThemes has a nice write-up on the new search and 3.7 in general here: http://rwdwp.com/50.

Handling Plugins

As you may have noticed in this chapter, plugins play an integral part in WordPress. They allow users and developers alike to extend the core functionality and, in many cases, do the heavy lifting for us. That's fantastic, but when it comes to choosing responsive-friendly plugins, there are some things we need to keep in mind.

LOADING FILES

NOTE
The fact that plugins aren't reviewed after the first submission means that developers could add some bad code later. The WordPress community is great about removing these issues, but it's always good to be cautious.

While there is a set of plugin development guidelines (http://rwdwp.com/51) and an initial code review for WordPress plugins submitted to the official directory, any future updates are not reviewed. That means it's up to developers and users to do some grunt work and read reviews, do some testing, and, if possible, check out the code. The biggest threat to good RWD when it comes to plugins is loading too many files or loading the wrong files.

For example, in exploring AJAX comment plugins for this chapter, there were several candidates that either didn't enqueue the JavaScript properly or loaded an old version of jQuery. In both cases, this can not only lead to conflict, but it can also lead to users downloading a lot more than they need to. The same thing goes for CSS.

At the very least, a plugin should offer an option in the theme to include the plugin's default style sheet or not. Perhaps as a developer you've included your own CSS to style the plugin's elements; loading the plugin's CSS would not only override yours but, again, unnecessarily bloat the page. This is another thing to consider when choosing a plugin.

NOTE
Really, most plugins shouldn't load more than one style sheet (though it may load an admin-specific one on the admin only). Make sure to check for superfluous style rules and ones that could override your site's CSS.

PROPER CODING CONVENTIONS

Over on the Codex, there are some coding conventions and suggestions for plugin development (http://rwdwp.com/52). While these don't pertain strictly to RWD, properly coded plugins can make a big difference.

Aside from properly loading files, using the proper markup, using the minimum amount of markup, and using widely supported markup are all important for plugins. Ideally, you should be able to assume that plugins and themes work well in all major browsers, but you should still test to make sure.

Finally, a good plugin will apply CSS classes (classes, NOT ids) to whatever HTML it generates. This allows you as the developer to apply whatever CSS you'd like. This may not always be possible—for example, content sliders are generally pretty dependent on the default CSS—but the plugin developer should do his best, as well as make sure his reasoning is well documented.

Obviously, putting every plugin you look at through the wringer would take an incredible amount of time; but as you load plugins, performance testing and browser testing certainly doesn't hurt. In fact, finding problems and reporting them to the developers make for better plugins for everyone.

Properly Testing Your Design

Testing a responsive website can be quite a cumbersome task. Whereas before, you could test on a couple of computers and a handful of browsers, now there are countless devices and browsers to test on. We will go into more detail about this in Chapter 6, but here are some quick notes on the topic

The nuts and bolts of it is that on top of desktop testing, you should test on a wide range of devices (including several Android and iOS devices; don't just pick one or two) and popular mobile browsers. This includes the default browsers, as well as Chrome, Opera, Opera Mini, and Dolphin. Finally, it's also important to do a speed test. Test on good Wi-Fi and bad Wi-Fi, 4G, 3G, and EDGE if you can find it.

While this is a lot of work for one person, there are solutions. One is doing a "private" beta by sending a link to friends, family, and followers to do some testing. There are also Open Device Labs popping up all over, allowing you to test on several devices all in one place: http://rwdwp.com/53.

Wrapping Up

Between this chapter and Chapter 4, we covered a lot of code and techniques to make WordPress themes responsive, while taking advantage of the tools WordPress has to offer by default. Both RWD and WordPress are constantly evolving (no doubt, by the time this book is out there will also be a new version of WordPress!), so it's important to stay on top of new developments.

Following the principles laid out throughout the book and applying them to these techniques and more should give you a solid foundation to work on. There are also countless other implementations out there, so experiment and see what you can come up with!

In the next chapter, we will take a small step back from RWD and talk about software reuse, frameworks, and more. These principles can then be applied to your responsive sites.

On Updating WordPress

WordPress is on a pretty aggressive release cycle, doing major version releases 2-3 times per year and frequent smaller releases (called "dot releases") as needed to fixes bugs and patch security issues.

It's very, very important to keep WordPress up to date, especially with the dot releases, because they will save you a lot of headaches if there are security patches that need to be fixed.

Since 3.7, WordPress will do dot releases automatically unless you or your hosting company configure it not to. I would strongly recommended keeping this feature on since it really is just fixes and security patches being pushed. No current code should break with these updates.

Questions

1. What are three responsive-friendly implementations for comments?

2. Why might a more visual implementation of tag clouds be better for mobile?

3. Why is a search bar an important element of an archives page?

4. Why is it important to check and test plugins?

Answers

1. Pagination, incremental loading, and a separate comments page.

2. It provides better UX for people whose full attention might not be on their mobile device.

3. This will likely be the first place users go, especially if they are looking for specific content.

4. If plugins are not coded properly or are doing something that isn't responsive-friendly, your users will have a bad experience.

Chapter **6**

Using Responsive Theme Frameworks

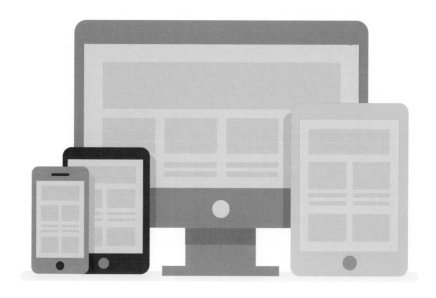

A recurring theme throughout this book—and in WordPress development in general—is the idea of separation of concerns. This is the notion that a computer program (or website, or app) should be broken up into parts that each address some issue. WordPress applies this idea by separating features from content from display. This allows users to easily change themes, add and remove functionality, and more. This is a form of reuse, the practice of creating components in code that are general enough to be used in several different programs. If you've ever copied and pasted code from one website to another, you've practiced software reuse; it's incredibly important in programming for many reasons: easier testing, saving time, the ability to focus on more advanced features, and so on. It's one of the most important things I learned while pursuing my master's degree at the University of Scranton. Then, once I graduated and entered the wonderful world of full-time freelancing, I decided I would need to apply those reuse lessons to my everyday life if I was going to keep doing WordPress work.

Some Principles of Reuse to Keep in Mind

Anyone with formal education in computer science or software engineering can attest to the fact that there are countless theories, libraries, and classes (programming classes, not academic classes) dedicated to some very advanced forms of reuse and generic programming. Volumes of books have been filled with those ideas, so I won't repeat them here, but there are some principles I tried to follow while considering reuse:

- ◆ **Design Your Code:** When talking about WordPress, design usually implies the front-end design, but it's just as important to design the code. Lay out what your functions, classes, and pages will be before you start to code them. Make sure you keep separation of concerns in mind, and that certain functions only do one thing. You want to minimize dependences or coupling.

- ◆ **Generalize When Possible:** Possibly the most important principle is to recognize when you're reusing code snippets and to generalize them into functions. This will make managing and updating your code much, much easier.

- ◆ **Document and Test Thoroughly:** This is something you should do with all code, but especially code you plan on reusing frequently. Documenting will help you remember what you were thinking six months or a year down the line. Testing will ensure that your code works before implementing it 5, 10, 100, or 1000 times.

Resource for Reuse

In general, software reuse consists of creating classes/objects and linking them together, where each class solves one (and only one) problem. There is also the idea of design patterns, which are defined as "formalized design practices." Essentially, these are pieces of code that create code on the fly, and they are at the heart of reuse. They go beyond the scope of this book, but a great resource if you want to learn more is the book *Design Patterns: Elements of Reusable Object-Oriented Software*, by Erich Gamma and colleagues.

Something that goes hand in hand with these principles is knowing what you want to program. When you create for clients, you want them to define their needs through a spec doc or RFP. It's just as important to do this when you create for yourself. This will allow you to adhere to the above principles.

Testing will ensure that your code works before implementing it 5, 10, 100, or even 1000 times.

On Device Testing

Up until this point, we've really focused on development techniques. One of the most important things to remember about responsive design, however, is that it's not just good enough to make sure your design shrinks with a smaller browser on your computer. Presumably, you're doing this because people will be accessing your website on mobile devices. Therefore, **you have to do device testing**! Here, I will outline what you should do to properly device-test your responsive sites.

This can be difficult since not everyone can get their hands on a wealth of devices. You may be lucky enough to be close to an Open Device Lab (http://rwdwp.com/53). If not, you should do your best to test on as many devices as possible. If you're an agency or firm that boasts about your RWD skills, you'll need to pony up and buy the devices. RWD isn't just a buzzword, and it needs to be done right.

Here's a list of the devices you absolutely need to test on; I'll try to keep it as general as possible since the device landscape is constantly changing.

◆ The current and previous generation of iPhones (with at least the two most recent versions of iOS)

◆ An iPad in each size (with at least the two most recent versions of iOS)

◆ Android 4.0+ Phones: The latest Nexus Phone, the latest Samsung Galaxy Note, the latest Samsung Galaxy S phone, the HTC Droid Incredible, the HTC Droid DNA or Razor Maxx, and the latest Motorola phone

◆ Android pre-4.0 Phones: Motorola Droid X, HTC Evo 4G

◆ Android Tablets: Nexus 7 and 10, Samsung Galaxy Note (10-inch), Galaxy Tab (8.9-inch), Kindle Fire, and a tablet running Honeycomb (3.0)

◆ At least one Blackberry (Q10, Z10)

◆ At least one Windows Phone (Nokia Lumia, HTC 8x)

◆ For fun: a Kindle or other e-Reader

Of course, do this at your discretion and based on your own analytics. If 0% of your users are using Gingerbread, pre-4.0 phones might not be an issue for you. This list for Android device testing is based on some cursory stat-searching, including Lifehacker's most common phones and stats directly from Google, which you can view on the Android Dashboards page (http://rwdwp.com/54) (**Figure 6.1**).

I understand that getting devices might be difficult. Luckily, Brad Frost provides a guide on how to cheaply get real devices for testing (http://rwdwp.com/56). You can also check out Swappa (http://rwdwp.com/57) for secondhand devices.

Figure 6.1
Lifehacker's most popular Android devices in mid-2013 (http://rwdwp.com/55)

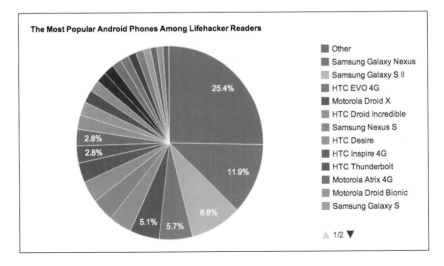

BROWSER TESTING

This should be nothing new, but with the whole host of new devices, it might be worthwhile to check out these browsers now:

◆ The device's native browser (e.g., Safari, Android's "Browser")

◆ Chrome on Android and iOS

◆ Mobile Opera

◆ Dolphin

◆ Mobile Firefox

Also, make sure to test in IE 8, 9, and 10! If you take a Mobile First approach, keep in mind that IE 8 does not support Media Queries. Finally, when it comes to RWD, device testing isn't the only aspect. You'll also need to consider speed.

SPEED TESTING

You cannot assume that everyone will have your great 70 Mbps connection (that's a real max speed for me at The University of Scranton). People could be getting less than 1 Mbps at times, and that's terrible if your site is huge. I would recommend testing on:

◆ Broadband (wired or Wi-Fi connection)

◆ 4G (on multiple carriers if possible)

◆ 3G (on multiple carriers if possible)

◆ 4G and 3G while traveling

I understand that this can be cumbersome and cause a lot of work, and admittedly I haven't been as diligent as I should be either. There are, however, ways you can do this sort of testing without breaking the bank. Aside from what Brad mentions, you can do things like an open or closed beta, inviting people with different devices and connections to test on their devices and report back. I will generally have my friends and coworkers test designs for me. Or you could always start an Open Device Lab. Now with testing covered, it's time to actually look at your needs.

Device and Browser Testing Services

All of this device and browser testing seems like a cumbersome task, but there are several tools out there that can help you. To do automated multi-device testing, there are two apps you can download that will hook into your browser and devices to display the same website on each device at the same time. The first is called Adobe Edge Inspect (http://rwdwp.com/58), which allows you to view the same website across several devices, take screenshots, do remote code inspection, and more. The second is Ghostlab (http://rwdwp.com/59), which offers many of the same features as Edge Inspect, but at a bit of a cheaper rate.

As for browsers, you don't necessarily need actual devices to get actual browser tests done. There are services online that will do screenshots of browsers for you. The first service has been around for quite a while and is called Browsershots (http://rwdwp.com/60). This is completely free but limited in functionality. If you want something with a bit more backbone, you can checkout BrowserStack (http://rwdwp.com/61). This service can be pricey but will get you lots of great features, including live tests, screenshots, and automation on hundreds of browsers.

Define Your Needs

Realizing I was reusing a theme over and over again, and testing the same things over and over, led me to create one very important piece of code: a theme framework that I use for all of my projects. Here you will go through the decision process for coding that theme. I recommend that you think about what you would want to get out of your own framework.

The first thing you'll need to do is define what you want your framework to accomplish. Remember that each of us has our own needs; while I'm going to talk about mine, yours may be different. My needs were fairly simple at first: I wanted a simple framework that did my initial work for me.

While creating WordPress themes for different clients, I noticed that my process was the same: Copy K2 (the default theme at the time), remove the stuff I don't want to use, and then replace it with my code. A lot of my code was similar: the same CSS reset, CSS structure, style header, navigation, and so on. After a while, I found it was easier just to copy my last client's theme and build on that. It was then that I decided to build my own framework.

With that decided, I needed to define my needs: What was I doing over and over again, and what could I generalize? My list of requirements was as follows:

Pluggable CSS: There are several parts of my CSS that rarely change. This includes WordPress class definitions, my CSS reset, some general classes I use (e.g., .hide, .left, .right, .clear), and (usually) my IE fixes. If I could abstract that all away, all I would need to do is dump it into style.css, and I know everything else would work properly. This would give me the opportunity to focus on doing the heavier lifting (and cooler stuff) instead of worrying about font sizes, padding, and more.

Constants for the Theme URL and Image Paths: These are two variables I need with every theme. If I could easily define them somewhere, I wouldn't need to worry about replacing the URLs for every site I create.

Common WordPress Functionality: This includes the menus, sidebar definitions, and anything else I could think of that I'd be typing over and over again.

Generally Defined Template Pages: These are common theme pages (header, footer, index) with enough on them to make them useful, but not so much on them that I'd have to really change the theme every time I developed a new theme.

Common Folders: I always have an images folder, css folder, and css/img folder. I had to include these too.

Lightweight: It's got to be lightweight. I don't want to have to sift through pages and pages of code to find what I want. My thought is that WordPress itself is a complex framework; why build a second complex framework on top?

I also wanted to build some functions for features of several pages, like the "page not found" message and the posts page navigation. This goes back to the mentality that a single function will help me more quickly change multi-page features.

EVOLUTION OF THE FRAMEWORK

Since I first defined my needs more than four years ago, they have changed and evolved (as they should). This is another lesson in reuse: Make sure to update and iterate! Nothing is bug free, and it's important to keep things up to date. Over the course of four years, I've used the framework in numerous projects that have led me to fix markup issues, optimize, and even generalize better. The first version of the framework wasn't even HTML5. Now it's fully responsive, and the starter font is a favorite from Google Web Fonts (http://rwdwp.com/62). The biggest changes have been to the functions.php file. I've even added a couple of functions thanks to the topics I covered in this book.

On Testing for WordPress

As mentioned in Chapter 5, WordPress gets major releases a couple of times in a year. While dot releases are often patches that don't need to be tested before you roll them out (though a backup wouldn't hurt), if you have any themes or plugins, it's important to test on the major releases. The new version will usually have a lead-time of one month to test, with Betas and Release Candidates (RCs) being released for developers to fix any issues that have surfaced. There is a great plugin that will allow you to easily install betas and nightly releases of WordPress called WordPress Beta Tester (http://rwdwp.com/63). I would recommend you only use this in test/development environments.

I've also learned better ways to debug, including some really nice print statements and `WP_DEBUG`, a constant designed to print error messages when set to `true`. It will inform you of PHP errors, database errors, and even when a function in WordPress is deprecated (or no longer used). To turn it on, open the wp-config.php file (in the root WordPress directory), and add this line:

```
define( 'WP_DEBUG', true );
```

It's important to remember to only use this in development copies of WordPress. You don't want errors being shown to users; this could make for a bad experience as well as be a big security risk.

The bottom line is this: If you build any type of reusable software (or any software, really), it's never done. It can always be refined.

SEE WHAT'S ALREADY OUT THERE

The fantastic thing about open source software, especially WordPress, is the great community of developers out there working on really great themes, plugins, and fixes to the Core. Because of that, there is almost always something already made that will fit your needs (or at least get you started). Before you start coding your own solution (something I've written about in various tutorials), it's worth looking at what's already out there.

In order to do that, take your list of needs, and compare them to the features offered by the tools you're looking at. There is one feature I didn't mention in my list of needs that will be very important in the search: It must be responsive.

As you may have guessed, in this chapter you are going to explore several responsive frameworks for WordPress. In many cases, using a popular framework is better than using your own homegrown one, because it sees widespread use and therefore is tested a lot more than something you would do on your own.

About WordPress Frameworks

In this chapter, we are going to look at several different frameworks that span across a couple of different categories. There are free and commercial frameworks, as well as WordPress-specific frameworks and frameworks retrofitted to work with WordPress.

There are also several sources for finding WordPress frameworks; as you can imagine, there are many different sources for WordPress-related products, but you should exercise some caution, as I'll explain below.

Finding Frameworks, Themes, and Even Plugins

This section isn't strictly about frameworks; it's equally about looking in the right places. Doing a simple Google search for "Free WordPress Themes" isn't going to cut it, because according to a study done by wpmu.org, most of what makes it to the first page includes themes with malicious code (http://rwdwp.com/64). But fear not! There are still many great sources out there for both free and commercial frameworks, themes, and plugins.

WORDPRESS.ORG

The first site is the WordPress directory (http://rwdwp.com/65), the official resource for open source themes. Automattic employees and high-ranking members of the WordPress community vet these themes when they are first submitted to the directory. Each theme is also ranked and reviewed by the community and displayed on the right sidebar (**Figure 6.2**).

Using these themes also offers the added bonus of being able to install and update them from right within the WordPress admin panel.

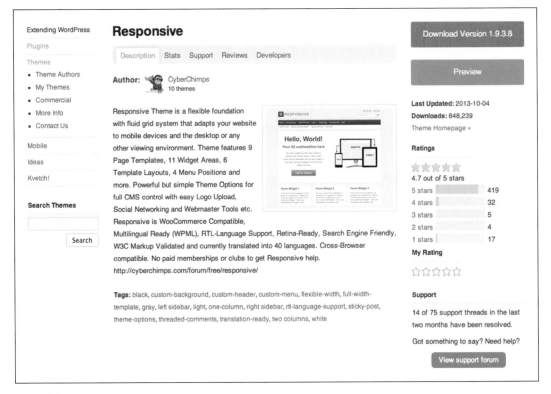

Figure 6.2
The "Responsive" theme in the WordPress directory. There is a description, a ranking, and a link to support forums.

THEMEFOREST

ThemeForest is a commercial marketplace owned by WordPress supporter Envato (http://rwdwp.com/66). They have a massive number of themes to choose from, and they organize those themes by category and tags. Like WordPress, ThemeForest reviews the code for every submission and even has a set of guidelines that developers need to follow (**Figure 6.3**).

One big problem with ThemeForest was that developers would feature-load themes to increase the value, but at the expense of creating high coupling between display and content. Luckily, the powers that be at Envato realized this and rewrote the guidelines to make sure themes handle only display (http://rwdwp.com/67).

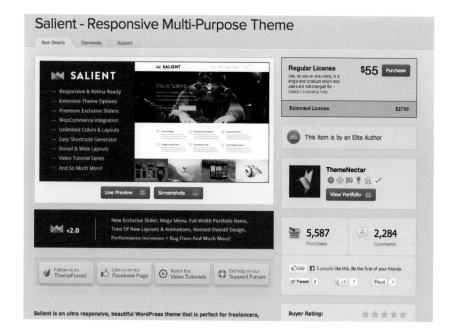

Figure 6.3 A theme on ThemeForest. The site includes metrics such as number of purchases, rating, and a comments section with support questions.

OTHERS

While those two are my favorite sources, there are many other great sources for WordPress themes.

Table 6.1

SITE	FREE/PAID	COMMENTS
Creative Market (http://rwdwp.com/68)	Paid	This is a relatively new site, but it is endorsed by WordPress.org due to its full GPL support.
WooThemes (http://rwdwp.com/69)	Both	A very popular and respected site that offers both free and paid themes.
Elegant Themes (http://rwdwp.com/70)	Paid	This is a one-time payment site that gives you access to many themes. It's well worth the money.
Roundups (e.g., *net Magazine*, *Smashing Magazine*)	Both	Many prominent websites will do roundups of the best WordPress themes. These are a great way to find themes, and I've listed several of them in the "Resources" section at the end of the book.

Why Use a Commercial Theme?

If there are so many great free resources, why bother paying for any WordPress tools at all? It's a valid question. In some cases, you may be getting the theme for free, but you're not guaranteed support, and the developer might disappear at any moment.

With commercial themes and plugins, you are more likely to get good customer support, faster bug fixes, and better updates. It also shows you that the developer is serious about development and that he is there for the long haul.

This is also how a lot of WordPress developers operate. Since you technically can't license WordPress, building out tools and providing great support for them is the closest WordPress will come to Software as a Service (SaaS). Some of the best themes and plugins are commercially run, and there's a reason for that: The developers are serious about creating these tools and making them work well.

Popular WordPress Frameworks

All right, let's get to it! There are quite a few theme frameworks to look at; remember that they must be responsive and that they should follow the guidelines listed above pretty well. First, let's look at some responsive frameworks that have been retrofitted to work with WordPress.

Bootstrap

This responsive framework has been widely popular ever since its release in 2011. Created by the fine folks at Twitter to solve inconsistencies in their code, it remains well-designed, lightweight, and easy to implement. And best of all, it's free (**Figure 6.4**).

Aside from being fully responsive (and developed Mobile First), Bootstrap successfully combines great CSS, a wide range of classes for alerts and buttons, and very well-integrated JavaScript effects that make doing a lot of things we've talked about in the book really easy.

This didn't start off as a WordPress theme, but a number of developers have tried their hand at making this framework WordPress-friendly. The most successful implementation seems to be WP-Bootstrap by 320press (http://rwdwp.com/71). Not only does this WordPress theme integrate the framework really well, but it also adds WordPress-specific features such as a theme options page for color schemes and fonts, and shortcodes for each button and alert box type.

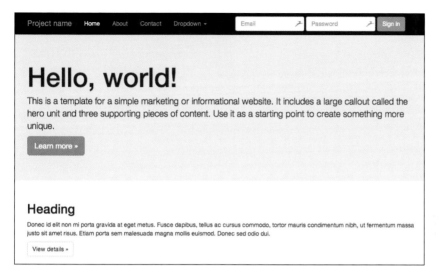

Figure 6.4 Jumbotron, a simple Bootstrap theme that showcases the big impact area with smaller content areas below.

Foundation

Foundation by ZURB is another popular beautifully designed site framework (http://rwdwp.com/72). Possibly touting more features than Bootstrap, Foundation is built on a flexible grid that makes it look great no matter what the screen size is (**Figure 6.5**).

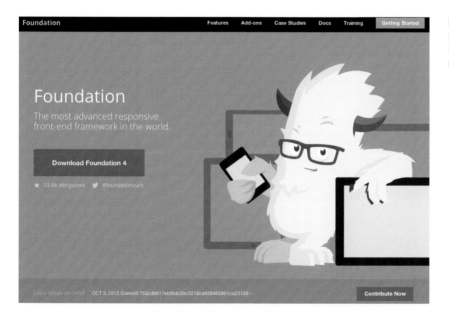

Figure 6.5 Foundation's homepage is built on a beautifully responsive framework.

Aside from looks, Foundation has a lot going on under the hood. It's got styles for buttons and boxes like Bootstrap, but it also touts its great styles for responsive forms and lengthy JavaScript component support. It does all of this with a total page weight of only 225 KB, which means it's a light download for users too. Finally, on the download page, you can actually customize the framework before downloading it, choosing the grid, font sizes, and more (**Figure 6.6**).

As for WordPress themes using the framework, they aren't as copious as they are on Bootstrap, but there is a really great contender out there called required+ (http://rwdwp.com/73). It integrates page templates, widget areas, and short-codes as far as the eye can see. It even goes so far as to add custom styles to the post editor.

If you're not sure how to choose between Bootstrap and Foundation, wpmu.org has a really great write-up about Foundation that includes several comparisons between the two, as well as a list of Foundation-based WordPress themes (http://rwdwp.com/74).

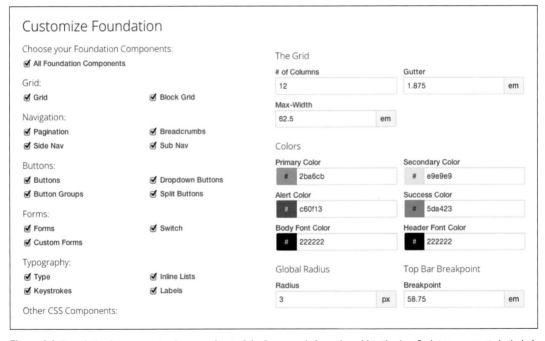

Figure 6.6 Foundation lets you customize every facet of the framework, from the grid to the JavaScript components included.

Honorable Mention: HTML5 Boilerplate

While Bootstrap and Foundation are the two titans in this arena, there is at least one more worth naming. HTML5 Boilerplate (http://rwdwp.com/75) is the framework that popularized HTML5 early on, and it's since been adapted to be responsive as well. There is a great community of developers behind it pushing it forward and showing us the best way to develop. A good WordPress theme that uses it is Boilerplate, which you'll find right in the WordPress Themes directory: http://rwdwp.com/76.

Aside from these HTML frameworks that developers converted to WordPress frameworks, there are a ton of frameworks out there created specifically for WordPress.

Thesis

Thesis (http://rwdwp.com/77) has been a very popular WordPress theme frame-work for a long time, and now it is fully responsive (**Figure 6.7**).

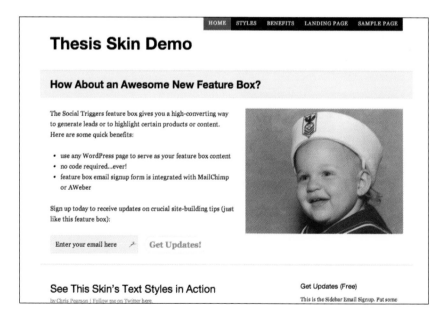

Figure 6.7 A screen shot of one of the designs offered by Thesis

Thesis offers an incredible number of features, including the ability to build out layouts from right within the WordPress admin. Through Skins, you can design full pages—HTML, CSS, images, and even a color scheme selector—all without code.

Through Boxes, Thesis allows you to add forms, social media buttons, mailing lists, and more. And through Site Tools, you can improve performance and optimize your site for search engines.

Beyond that, you can use Thesis as a parent theme, extending the functionality or changing up the look and feel. You'll have to pay, though: Thesis costs between $87 and $197.

Genesis

Genesis (http://rwdwp.com/78) is another WordPress framework that's been around for quite some time but got a revamp in 2013 to be responsive. It also received a very clean, crisp redesign (**Figure 6.8**).

While it doesn't tout as many features as Thesis does, this is much more a developer's framework. It serves as a very good base for building great themes. It also comes with a good number of page layouts and sidebar layouts.

This framework costs $59.99 and requires a membership at StudioPress, a popular marketplace that specializes in building Genesis-based themes.

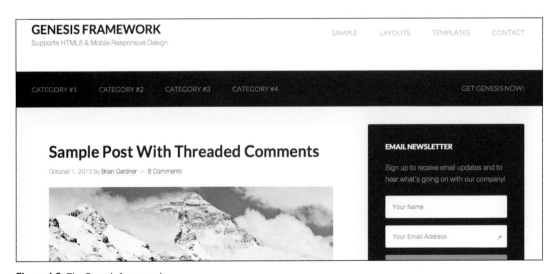

Figure 6.8 The Genesis framework

Underscores

Underscores or _s (http://rwdwp.com/79) is an open source, minimal WordPress framework released by none other than Automattic itself. It touts a bunch of features geared towards making it easy to start a theme without getting in the way. This includes well-commented HTML5 templates, multiple CSS layouts that are well-organized and easy to read, and more. There is even a script called navigation.js that mimics responsive-nav.js.

If you're looking for an official release that's a bit more feature-rich, however, Automattic has your back.

Twenty Thirteen

A few years ago, Automattic decided to make it a tradition to release a new default WordPress theme every year to showcase the new features of the latest build, as well as give users a starting point. It is always named after the year in which it was released; at the time of this writing, the theme is Twenty Thirteen (http://rwdwp.com/80) (**Figure 6.9**).

Figure 6.9 WordPress' default theme, Twenty Thirteen.

NOTE
By the time this book comes out, Twenty Fourteen will be in the works, even if it's not officially announced. Keep an eye out for it.

The theme is single column by design but allows for sidebar widgets and even integrates jQuery Masonry (http://rwdwp.com/81). The reason it's included here as a framework is because the developers encourage the use of this theme as a starting point, and they make it easy to create well-formed child themes using Twenty Thirteen as a parent.

USING CHILD/PARENT THEMES

If you're unfamiliar, a child theme is a theme that uses another theme as a base; that base is called the "parent." In order to use a theme as a parent, all you have to do is slightly modify the theme definition in style.css (emphasis added):

```
/*
Theme Name: Land O' Flights
Theme URI: http://milleniumflights.com
Description: A child theme based off of Millennium Flights'
→theme.
Version: 1.5
Template: millenniumflights
Author: Joe Casabona
Author URI: http://www.casabona.org
*/
```

NOTE
For more on how to develop a child theme, you can check out my tutorial at tutsplus.com: http://rwdwp.com/82

You'll notice the extra line in the definition for "Template," which must be the name of a folder in the /wp-content/themes/ directory. This tells WordPress where the parent theme is located. After importing the parent theme's CSS, you're ready to make modifications:

```
@import url("../millenniumflights/style.css");
```

The honest-to-goodness beauty of WordPress—and why I saved this part for last—is that because of parent and child themes, any theme can be a framework. A framework is simply defined as *a reusable software platform to develop applications.* In the case of child themes, we are reusing a parent theme. Keep that in mind next time you find a WordPress theme you really like. If it's done right, you can keep reusing that theme while continually making changes to it.

On Modifying Themes

There is another, more important reason to use child themes. If you do decide that you need to make modifications to a theme, a child theme is the way to go. This can be pretty common, especially if your client chooses one from a marketplace and wants you to adjust it for their colors and branding.

   If you modify the actual theme (or parent) and you update that theme, you will lose any changes you made and will have to start over. With a child theme, the parent can update while leaving your modifications intact.

Developing Your Own Theme Framework

While exploring these frameworks, keep your requirements in mind. Test frameworks properly. Download, install, and enable; try building a child theme and playing with the settings. See what you find, and then make your decision.

I felt that the ones I tried were too complex and not lightweight. They are great for users who need a theme quickly, but, as far as customizing goes, I had to learn a whole new system in order to build themes. I already know WordPress' complex framework/API. I'd have to replace that knowledge with another theme's framework/API. I decided to build my own, which would still use WordPress' functions, not replace them.

If you decide that you'd like to develop your own framework, remember to keep in mind both your needs and the principles of reuse. Make sure that what you build is general but usable on its own. Make sure to allow for growth, and, of course, test. A lot.

Wrapping Up

Software reuse is not something that is patently WordPress, but it is something that's found all throughout the WordPress platform. Developing general, reusable pieces of code, especially for themes, will make development 100 times easier because it automates a lot of the initial setup that tends to take a lot of time.

In this chapter, we explored several frameworks, including popular responsive ones like Bootstrap and Foundation. These two, in particular, are very popular because they are done right; they successfully execute many of the tenets of responsive design that we looked at in Chapter 1. Combining these with WordPress themes to make a solid responsive WordPress theme framework will guarantee the creation of some solid themes.

We also looked at a few WordPress theme frameworks and learned that any WordPress theme can be a framework thanks to parent-child themes. If you go off and create your own theme framework, remember this dynamic.

In the next chapter, we will take everything we've learned here, and we will apply those skills and principles in cookbook-style tutorials.

Questions

1. What is the name of the principle that each part of a computer program solves one problem/issue?
2. Why is just testing in the browser not good enough?
3. Name one valid source for downloading themes.
4. Why should you use child themes instead of modifying themes directly?

Answers

1. Separation of concerns
2. Users will be accessing your site on mobile devices; therefore, you must test on real devices.
3. Any of the following: WordPress.org, ThemeForest, WooThemes, Creative Market, Elegant Themes, roundups
4. If you update a modified theme, you will lose the modifications.

Chapter **7**

Techniques
and Tutorials

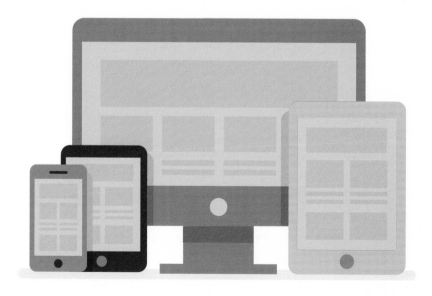

Introduction

So you've just spent an entire book looking at responsive design and WordPress, including themes, plugins, different design patterns, and more; you can leverage WordPress' inherent functionality to make your responsive themes more efficient. Now it's time to look at some tutorials that will give you step-by-step instructions on how to create some frequently used features.

Moving forward, it's important to remember that while you can use any of this code in a theme or a plugin, you should consider how what you're building is being used. For example, since a portfolio is inherently content, you shouldn't make it part of the theme, because when you change the theme you lose the content. At the beginning of each tutorial, I will make a recommendation as to where I would place the code.

Most of them will be some sort of combination, actually. The functionality, or core code, will be in a plugin—things like portfolios, products, and contact forms lend themselves well to plugins—and you'll use either shortcodes or template pages for displaying the information. I'll be guiding you through five different tutorials:

- Photo Gallery — Theme using WordPress' built-in media gallery
- Google Map — Theme using shortcode
- Image Slider — Plugin/shortcode
- Contact Form — Plugin/shortcode
- Products — Plugin/shortcode

Focus On: CPTs and CSS

As you can imagine, the main focus is going to be on the CSS. Since it's important to make each of these features as light as possible, though, you'll see instances of RESS, picturefill, and other tools we looked at in the book. But as far as displaying it goes, CSS reigns supreme.

The other focus of this section will be Custom Post Types (CPTs). In most cases, the process for development will follow the same steps:

1. Plan out the Post Type.
2. Build and register the Post Type.

3. Write a display function or shortcode.

4. Create the template (if needed).

5. Write the CSS.

As I was creating these tutorials, I kept these questions in mind; I would recommend that you think about them as well:

◆ **Does this look good across multiple devices and browsers?** I know it's tough to test everything, but test as much as you can.

◆ **Do I properly adjust at the right places?** This will be the hardest thing to follow in the upcoming tutorials. I'll do my best to create breakpoints for the content, but this will vary from theme to theme.

◆ **Am I loading any unnecessary scripts or files?** This is something that can happen easily in WordPress. Make sure to properly use `enqueue_script()` to ensure that you're not loading something WordPress already loaded. I would also advise against loading extra CSS files when you can avoid it. Remember: the more files you have, the more requests you're asking the user to make.

◆ **Does my code encroach on anyone else's?** Make sure you use prefixes and other WordPress best practices to avoid conflicts that will potentially break WordPress websites.

Finally, one thing that isn't covered in these tutorials is the inclusion of proper documentation for themes and plugins. If you plan on releasing anything to either official WordPress directory (or any marketplace for that matter), you should make sure your functions are properly documented and your README file is in order. Make sure to list any CSS classes—as well as what they do and variable names—so users don't have to hunt for that information. You can find more information on this here: http://wordpress.org/plugins/about/readme.txt

It's worth noting that since these are one-off tutorials, we won't necessarily be using The Millennium Flights theme that was used throughout the rest of the book. Feel free to use anything you'd like. For functions, the prefix `mf_` will still be used for simplicity and consistency.

With all of this in mind, let's get started!

NOTE

Don't feel obligated to use my breakpoints. If you have better ones that apply to your theme, definitely use them.

NOTE

When it comes to documenting functions, I would recommend using phpdoc. You can quickly and easily generate documentation based on comments preceding your functions: http://rwdwp.com/83

How to Build a Responsive WordPress Photo Gallery

NOTE

This was developed using WordPress 3.6. In new releases, the Media Manager is due to see some big improvements.

There are a number of plugins out there to manage photos in WordPress, including ones that hook into other services like Flickr. In recent years, however, WordPress has significantly improved its media manager and makes it incredibly easy to manage photos and create galleries by adding pictures to a page or post. In this tutorial, you'll look at adding a gallery through the WordPress editor, and then styling it to be responsive.

Creating a Gallery from New Images

WordPress makes this incredibly easy. First open up a page or post in the editor, and click the "Add Media" button to upload however many images you'd like (**Figure 7.1**).

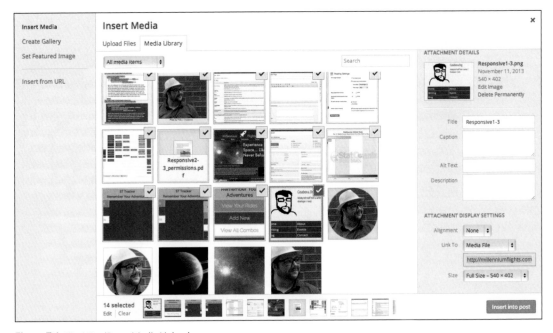

Figure 7.1 The WordPress Media Uploader.

Once you've uploaded the images, there are two ways to add a gallery. You can use the "Create Gallery" area of the Media Uploader, which will give you greater control over what images are included, or you can use the shortcode that the "Create Gallery" area generates. The shortcode looks something like this:

```
[gallery link="file" columns="3"]
```

You can choose the number of columns, which photos to use, and whether you want to link directly to the file or to the attachment page, which is a template page in WordPress. The id attribute, which accepts a comma-delimited list of photo IDs, is not shown, because all of the images added to the page will be shown.

TIP
Linking to the file makes it easier to use overlay libraries like lightbox.

Once your gallery is ready to go, simply publish it out and visit the page. The page looks nice, divided into however many columns you decided on, but the page is not responsive. Further, if you look at the source, you'll see that CSS was injected right into the page body:

```
#gallery-1 {
    margin: auto;
}
#gallery-1 .gallery-item {
    float: left;
    margin-top: 10px;
    text-align: center;
    width: 33%;
}
#gallery-1 img {
    border: 2px solid #cfcfcf;
}
#gallery-1 .gallery-caption {
    margin-left: 0;
}
```

Adding CSS to your style.css file will not work, because it will be overridden by the inline code. Luckily, there is a hook in WordPress that allows you to modify the CSS: gallery_style.

Changing the CSS

The process here is two steps, and it seems to first have been implemented in Twenty Ten, WordPress' default theme, introduced in 2010. The first step is to use a regular expression to remove the inline style and the line breaks, which is where the hooks come in, and then add the styles to the theme's style sheet using these classes generated by WordPress:

```
.gallery {} //Styles the whole image gallery
.gallery-item {} //Styles each column (default is a <dl>)
.gallery-icon {} //Styles each thumbnail (default is a <dt>)
.gallery-caption {} //Styles each caption (default is a <dd>)
```

It would be a good idea to remember the CSS above, since it's fairly similar to what the full-width CSS will look like.

The first step is to remove the inline CSS and line breaks using these functions/filters:

```
function mf_gallery_style($css){
    return preg_replace("#<style type=\'text/css\'>(.*?)
    →</style>#s", "", $css);
}

add_filter( 'gallery_style', 'mf_gallery_style');

function mf_remove_br_gallery($output) {
    return preg_replace('/<br style=(.*)>/mi','',$output);
}

add_filter( 'the_content', 'mf_remove_br_gallery', 11, 2);
```

They are both one-liners that do regex find/replace and returns theme. The first one looks for anything starting at `<style type=\'text/css\'>` and ending at `</style>`. The function is called when the filter `gallery_style` is triggered. The second filters the content, looking for any `<br>` elements that have inline CSS attached. That's because the gallery function automatically adds these based on the number of columns, which will cause problems as the user's screen width increases. They will essentially add a maximum limit on the number of columns no matter how wide a user's screen gets.

Now that the gallery is CSS-less and br-less, it's time to add your own styles, which will happen in style.css. You'll start with the smaller screens, which means there's not a whole lot you need to do.

```
.gallery{
    margin: 0 auto;
    text-align: center;
    }

.gallery img{
    max-width: 100%;
    }

.gallery-icon img{
    border: 1px solid #CCCCCC;
    background: #FFFFFF;
    padding: 5px;
    }
```

There is some groundwork that's laid here to ensure that the images resize properly, as well as some padding and a background added to images; you can, of course, use any color you like for your background. One note: the reason the background color is added to the image and not the .gallery-item class is that the class extends the full width of the browser, not just the image.

Expanding out, you'll want to do things like line up the images, one next to another. Choose your breakpoints at your own discretion. Mine are based on my template.

```
@media screen and (min-width: 25.313em){
    .gallery-icon{
        float: left;
        margin: 10px 2%;
        width: 45%;
        }
    }
```

This (and the rest of the) CSS is fairly simple. Now that you've removed breaks, you can move your gallery to a two-column layout by floating each image container and changing the width; the base CSS will do the rest. The CSS for three- and four-column layouts will look similar:

```
@media screen and (min-width: 51.5em){
    .gallery-icon{
        width: 30%;
        margin: 10px 1%;
        }
    }

@media screen and (min-width: 76.625em){
    .gallery-icon{
        width: 22%;
        }
    }
```

Here you are just adjusting the size of the `.gallery-icon` items as the page width expands. Not too shabby, right? Now you have a completely responsive photo gallery using WordPress' built-in gallery (**Figure 7.2**).

Figure 7.2 Here is the responsive gallery, with both the "full width" layout and a mobile device display shown in the inset.

Using Photo Gallery Plugins

If you want to have more control over the customization of your photo gallery, or want more robust functionality, several good plugins are up to the task. Doing a cursory search in the WordPress Plugin Directory will yield some good results (http://rwdwp.com/85), but my recommendation is NextGen Gallery (http://rwdwp.com/86)

   This plugin will let you upload, manipulate, and organize images in several ways, including creating galleries and albums, which contain multiple galleries. You can also create templates for how those galleries are displayed using NextGen's template tags. This gives developers a massive amount of flexibility without having to undo what's already there.

Caveat

So far, this tutorial hasn't accounted for captions. The default markup for the gallery isn't that great for RWD (at the time of this writing). It uses individual definition lists (`<dl>`) for each photo/caption pair and the definition tags (`<dt>`, `<dd>`) to list the image and the caption, which makes independent styling more complicated. Further, it inserts inline CSS and manual line breaks (which we fix using the code above). Using the right markup would take some extensive coding, recoding, and hacky CSS. Luckily, there is the `gallery_shortcode` function that prints out the entire markup for the gallery and accepts some limited arguments for customization. There is also the ability to change the function called by the shortcode, as follows:

```
remove_shortcode('gallery', 'gallery_shortcode');
add_shortcode('gallery', 'my_gallery_shortcode');
```

These two lines of code will allow you to write your own output function by changing the shortcode from calling WordPress' built-in function to calling your own function. They are both advanced beyond the scope of this tutorial, but the function is available online here: http://rwdwp.com/84.

It's recommended that you copy the output of WordPress' function into your own function and start modifying where the output starts, somewhere around line 782. My approach would be to create some markup like this:

```
<div class="gallery-item">
<div class="gallery-img">
        <img src="photo.jpg" alt="alt text" />
</div>
    <div class="gallery-img-caption">
        This is the caption
    </div>
</div>
```

Then you could set a width and float on the entire gallery-item while keeping the image and caption together.

How to Build a Responsive WordPress Map Page Using Google Maps

Google Maps appear frequently on websites of all kinds, and there are actually a number of plugins out there to help integrate Google Maps into WordPress sites. That said, this tutorial will look at the use of shortcodes and, more importantly, how to make Google Maps (and other iframe-based content such as YouTube videos) responsive.

This will be done in two steps: Create a shortcode to easily add a Google Map to a page, and then add the CSS to make the map responsive. It will all be done within the theme, and the end result will be something like what's shown in **Figure 7.3**.

Figure 7.3 A responsive WordPress map page using Google Maps, shown on both desktop and mobile.

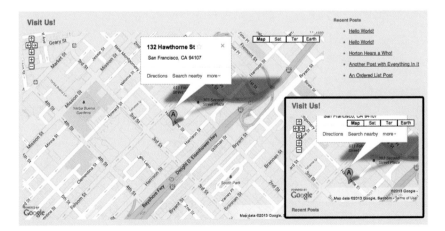

Creating the Shortcode

The first step is to create a shortcode that will allow users to place the map right into the WordPress editor. You can do this with this block of code in the functions.php file:

```php
add_shortcode('mf_gmap', 'mf_google_maps');

function mf_google_maps($atts, $content=null){
        //extract arguments from shortcode
        extract(shortcode_atts(array('address' => '132 Hawthorne
        ↪Street San Francisco, CA 94107', 'width' => 800,
        ↪'height' => 600), $atts));
        $map= '<div class="mf-responsive-map"><iframe
        ↪width="'.$width.'" height="'.$height.'"
        ↪frameborder="0" scrolling="no" marginheight="0"
        ↪marginwidth="0" src="https://www.google.com/maps?q=
        ↪'.$address.'&output=embed"></iframe>';
        if($content != null){
            $map.= '<br/>'.$content;
        }
        $map.= "</div>";

        return $map;
}
```

NOTE

It's actually recommended in HTML5 to use CSS for height, width, frameborder, scrolling, marginheight, and marginwidth. They are kept in the tutorial to illustrate the use of shortcode arguments and because this is the output from maps.google. com. For more information, see http://rwdwp. com/87.

There are a few activities happening here. In the first line, add_shortcode ('mf_gmap', 'mf_google_maps'), we are registering the shortcode with WordPress. The first argument is the shortcode itself—that is, what will go in the editor. Ours will be [mf_gmap]. The second argument is the callback function, which will be used to generate the map.

In our function, mf_google_maps(), you will notice that two arguments are accepted. The first is $atts, which is an array of attributes that we can send with the shortcode. For example: [mf_gmap width=640]. In this case, width is the attribute and 640 is the value (in this case, a width as pixels is assumed). The attributes are sent as an associative array.

The second argument, $content, is any content in between the opening and closing tag, which WordPress automatically looks for. So, for example, in [mf_gmap]Find Your Place[/mf_gmap], the content would be "Find Your Place."

The first line of the function does the heavy lifting. It extracts any arguments that you send with the shortcode while simultaneously assigning default values. The built-in WordPress function `shortcode_atts()` will handle all of that with two arguments; the first is an array of key => value pairs the function will look for. If you pass an argument that is not specifically mentioned in the array, WordPress will ignore it. As you can see, there are three variables we are looking for:

◆ `address`: This will be the address we send as a query string to Google Maps. The default value is *132 Hawthorne Street San Francisco, CA 94107* (home to none other than Automattic, the driving force behind WordPress).

◆ `width`: The default width, which we set to 800px. This will actually be completely ignored, but you'll need to include it to ensure that the iframe functions properly.

◆ `height`: The default height, which we set to 600px. Again, this will be ignored.

NOTE

Unless you're in a controlled section of code (like a function) and know what variables are in the array, you shouldn't use `extract()`. It can break things.

The second argument you'll pass to `shortcode_atts()` is the list of attributes, `$atts`. The PHP `extract()` function creates variables out of the key => value pairs, so we can do `$address` instead of `$atts['address']`.

After that, you'll create your map using Google Maps' standard iframe setup. You'll use your variables to fill in the blanks, and if there's any content, you'll print it after the map (this is usually where "View Larger Map" goes). Then, you'll return the map. This is very important! If you don't do this, our shortcode will be removed and nothing will be put in its place. When creating shortcode functions, it's very important to remember to return, not print.

With that, the shortcode is complete. You should be able to go to the WordPress editor and do something similar to what is pictured in **Figure 7.4**.

Figure 7.4 Using the shortcode in the editor.

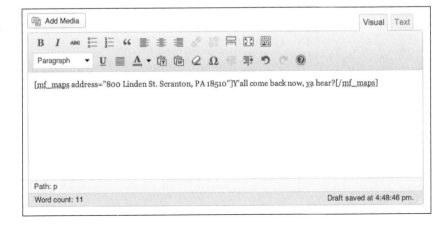

If you do this and head out to your site, you might notice that the map is 800x600, regardless of resizing the browser. That's because the CSS hasn't been added yet. Open up style.css, and add these lines in a **non-media query-specific area:**

```
.mf-responsive-map {
    position: relative;
    padding-bottom: 56.25%;
    padding-top: 30px;
    height: 0;
    overflow: hidden;
}

.mf-responsive-map iframe,
.mf-responsive-map  object,
.mf-responsive-map  embed {
    position: absolute;
    top: 0;
    left: 0;
    width: 100%;
    height: 100%;
}
```

Notice that in the shortcode function, we are wrapping the map in a div with the class `mf-responsive-map`. That is so we can apply a sort of hack that allows iframes to maintain aspect ratio as the browser changes size. This actually employs a fix that has been around for a while (since 2009 at least).

That's it! Save your work and check it out. You should get results similar to the screenshots above.

If you want to expand your shortcode, you could always add more arguments, or if you're really familiar with Google Maps, change the map generated from the standard iframe to one using the Google Maps API.

How to Build a Responsive WordPress Image Slider

I'm going to admit two things here: First, I'm not a big fan of content sliders. I can see why they became really popular (especially with people thinking in terms of the elusive "fold"), but I think people who are using them force unnecessary interactions on the part of the user. Image sliders are a bit different, and while I don't personally use them often (on my own sites at least), I can see why people do.

The second admission is that I am actually kind of cheating in this tutorial. You're going to build a plugin around a slider that is responsive right out of the box: FlexSlider. I've been using it for a few years now, and I really like it. If you'd like, you can give it a try with another slider; the process should be basically the same. So what is the process?

1. Providing basic definitions of the plugin and variables

2. Including the slider scripts

3. Building a shortcode and template tag to include the slider

4. Building the CPT to add images from the WordPress admin (**Figure 7.5**)

Figure 7.5 The end result (or something like it).

Definition of Plugin and Variables

I won't spend too much time on this section since code has been covered quite a bit in this book. First, create a directory and file of the same name within the /plugins/ directory. Then add these lines of code:

```
/*
Plugin Name: Responsive Image Slider
Plugin URI: http://millenniumflights.com
Description: A simple plugin that integrates FlexSlider
→(http://flex.madebymufffin.com/) with WordPress using
→custom post types!
Author: Joe Casabona
Version: 1.0
Author URI: http://www.casabona.org
*/

/*Some Set-up*/
define('MFS_PATH', WP_PLUGIN_URL . '/' .
→plugin_basename( dirname( __FILE__ ) ) . '/' );
define('MFS_NAME', "Responsive Image Slider");

/*Files to Include*/
require_once('mf-image-slider-cpt.php');
```

In the first few lines, we have the plugin definition, a couple of constants for later use, and one required file, which is where the CPT will be defined.

Including the Slider Scripts

Next, it's time to add the JavaScript and CSS. If you haven't already, download FlexSlider from http://rwdwp.com/88, and add the following to your plugin: jquery.flexslider-min.js and flexslider.css. Make sure both are in the folder's root. Then add the following code:

```
function mfs_enqueue_scripts(){
    wp_enqueue_script('mf-image-slider', MFS_PATH.'jquery.
    →flexslider-min.js', array('jquery'));
    wp_enqueue_style('mf-image-slider-css', MFS_PATH.
    →'flexslider.css');
}

add_action('wp_enqueue_scripts', 'mfs_enqueue_scripts');

function mfs_script(){

    print '<script type="text/javascript" charset="utf-8">
        jQuery(window).load(function() {
            jQuery(".flexslider").flexslider();
        });
    </script>';

}

add_action('wp_head', 'mfs_script');
```

This should all look pretty standard to you; there's the call to `wp_enqueue_script`, where the FlexSlider jQuery plugin will be included, the inclusion of CSS for FlexSlider, and a function (`mfs_script`) that will print the jQuery function to make your FlexSlider work. It will be printed in the head, as `add_action` is being called with the hook `wp_head`.

One thing I want to point out is the `wp_enqueue_style` line. This will load another style sheet, therefore increasing the number of HTTP requests the site is making, which is using more of the user's resources. As performance is a chief concern of RWD, I have been opting to comment that line out and include the CSS in my single style.css file to lower the number of requests. While I don't cover it here, if I were to release this plugin for use, I would include an options page that allowed users to exclude this call, as well as give them the CSS to copy and paste into their style.css file. The only pitfall of this approach is now the plugin is slightly dependent on the theme. However, the user has control over this and can choose to use the plugin's default code.

The Shortcode and Template Tag

With WordPress handling the JavaScript and CSS, it's time to give users a way to include the slider on their pages and in their themes. Before creating the shortcode or template tag, what you should do is create a single output function that both the shortcode and template tag can call:

```
function mfs_get_slider(){
    $slider= '<div class="flexslider">
      <ul class="slides">';

    $args= "post_type=slider-image";
    $slides= new WP_Query($args);


     while($slides->have_posts()) : $slides->the_post();
        $img= get_the_post_thumbnail( $post->ID, 'large' );

        $slider.='<li>'.$img.'
               <p class="flex-caption"><strong>'.
               ⇥get_the_title() .'</strong><br/>'.
               ⇥get_the_content() .'</p>
        </li>';

    endwhile;

    wp_reset_postdata();
    $slider.= '</ul>
    </div>';

    return $slider;
}
```

This function is the main driver for the plugin. It uses `WP_Query` to grab each slider from the CPT that you'll create later. Notice that `get_posts` isn't used. That's because it can cause a conflict with the Main Loop. Instead, you're using `WP_Query` and then calling `wp_reset_postdata()` when this Loop is complete. As you can see, we're grabbing the "large" featured image (which we'll define later), and we're making the title and content the caption for the slide.

Finally, you should also notice that the markup is being stored in a variable and returned. You might recall from the Google Maps tutorial that shortcodes need to return something to work properly, so returning a variable now will give us the most flexibility later. With that, both the shortcode and template tags are very simple:

```
/**The Shortcode**/
function mfs_shortcode($atts, $content=null){

    $slider= mfs_get_slider();

    return $slider;

}

add_shortcode('mf_slider', 'mfs_shortcode');

/**The Template Tag**/
function mfs_slider_tag(){

    print mfs_get_slider();
}
```

It should now be apparent why `mfs_get_slider` returns instead of prints. It is called in both the shortcode and template tag functions. You'll notice that the shortcode function accepts no attributes; the slider will print with all of the default settings. Since the template tag is just a function users can put into their themes, we just use the tag to print what we are already saving in `mfs_get_slider`.

Building the Custom Post Type

The CPT for this plugin will be very simple; in fact, it's no more than 25 lines, to be added to mf-image-slider-cpt.php:

TIP
Since we are using
get_the_post_
thumbnail(),
you can use the
function/hook
from Chapter 4 to
insert picturefill
for this plugin.
However, results
may vary due to
how FlexSlider
handles resizing
the div.

```php
<?php
define('MFS_CPT_NAME', "Slider Images");
define('MFS_CPT_SINGLE', "Slider Image");
define('MFS_CPT_TYPE', "slider-image");
add_theme_support('post-thumbnails', array('slider-image'));

function mfs_register() {
    $args = array(
        'label' => __(MFS_CPT_NAME),
        'singular_label' => __(MFS_CPT_SINGLE),
        'public' => true,
        'show_ui' => true,
        'capability_type' => 'post',
        'hierarchical' => false,
        'rewrite' => true,
        'supports' => array('title', 'editor', 'thumbnail')
        );

    register_post_type(MFS_CPT_TYPE , $args );
}


add_action('init', 'mfs_register');

?>
```

I've gotten into the habit of creating constants for the labels and slugs for my CPTs so that they are easy to reference consistently later. As you can see, we are adding thumbnail support and then registering the CPT. Once this is completed, you're all set! You should now see a section in the WordPress admin called Slider Images. Create a post with a title, text in the editor, and then add a featured image and save. Once you add a few you can go to a page and use the shortcode, or add the template tag right into your theme.

I would add a couple of recommendations: Earlier in the book, I showed you a couple of methods for implementing picturefill.js. I would suggest you use one of the methods here to make your sliders a little lighter for mobile users. I would also encourage you to add your own CSS for the slider and captions to make them stylistically like your site.

If you want to extend this plugin a bit, you can also add attributes to the shortcode for all of the customizable features in FlexSlider. You can view a list by visiting http://rwdwp.com/88, scrolling down to "Get Started," and clicking the "Advanced" tab (**Figure 7.6**).

Figure 7.6 All of the advanced settings for FlexSlider.

All available FlexSlider properties

This was mentioned in the Get Started tab, but it is worth reiterating. Listed below are all of the options available to customize FlexSlider to suite your needs, along with their default values.

```
namespace: "flex-",              //{NEW} String: Prefix string attached
selector: ".slides > li",        //{NEW} Selector: Must match a simple p
animation: "fade",               //String: Select your animation type, "
easing: "swing",                 //{NEW} String: Determines the easing me
direction: "horizontal",         //String: Select the sliding direction,
reverse: false,                  //{NEW} Boolean: Reverse the animation
animationLoop: true,             //Boolean: Should the animation loop?
smoothHeight: false,             //{NEW} Boolean: Allow height of the sl
startAt: 0,                      //Integer: The slide that the slider sh
slideshow: true,                 //Boolean: Animate slider automatically
slideshowSpeed: 7000,            //Integer: Set the speed of the slidesh
animationSpeed: 600,             //Integer: Set the speed of animations,
initDelay: 0,                    //{NEW} Integer: Set an initialization
randomize: false,                //Boolean: Randomize slide order

// Usability features
pauseOnAction: true,             //Boolean: Pause the slideshow when int
pauseOnHover: false,             //Boolean: Pause the slideshow when hov
useCSS: true,                    //{NEW} Boolean: Slider will use CSS3 t
touch: true,                     //{NEW} Boolean: Allow touch swipe navi
video: false,                    //{NEW} Boolean: If using video in the

// Primary Controls
controlNav: true,                //Boolean: Create navigation for paging
directionNav: true,              //Boolean: Create navigation for previo
prevText: "Previous",            //String: Set the text for the "previou
nextText: "Next",                //String: Set the text for the "next" d

// Secondary Navigation
keyboard: true,                  //Boolean: Allow slider navigating via
multipleKeyboard: false,         //{NEW} Boolean: Allow keyboard navigat
mousewheel: false,               //{UPDATED} Boolean: Requires jquery.mo
pausePlay: false,                //Boolean: Create pause/play dynamic el
pauseText: 'Pause',              //String: Set the text for the "pause"
playText: 'Play',                //String: Set the text for the "play" p

// Special properties
controlsContainer: "",           //{UPDATED} Selector: USE CLASS SELECTO
manualControls: "",              //Selector: Declare custom control navi
sync: "",                        //{NEW} Selector: Mirror the actions pe
asNavFor: "",                    //{NEW} Selector: Internal property exp

// Carousel Options
itemWidth: 0,                    //{NEW} Integer: Box-model width of ind
itemMargin: 0,                   //{NEW} Integer: Margin between carouse
minItems: 0,                     //{NEW} Integer: Minimum number of caro
maxItems: 0,                     //{NEW} Integer: Maxmimum number of car
move: 0,                         //{NEW} Integer: Number of carousel ite

// Callback API
start: function(){},             //Callback: function(slider) - Fires wh
before: function(){},            //Callback: function(slider) - Fires as
after: function(){},             //Callback: function(slider) - Fires af
end: function(){},               //Callback: function(slider) - Fires wh
added: function(){},             //{NEW} Callback: function(slider) - Fi
removed: function(){}            //{NEW} Callback: function(slider) - Fi
```

How to Build a Responsive WordPress Contact Form

There are a great many WordPress plugins available for forms. Everything from Ninja Forms (http://rwdwp.com/89), which you can find in the Plugin Directory, to the great Gravity Forms (http://rwdwp.com/90), which is well worth the money because of all the features it offers, from its great GUI to its entry management to its e-commerce features.

In fact, when it comes to responsive forms, the onus is on the CSS to ensure that it behaves properly; you can really use any contact form plugin you'd like, as well as write your own. In this tutorial, I'm going to use Contact Form 7 (http://rwdwp.com/91). It's really simple and is driven primarily by your own markup.

The goal here is to make sure the CSS for the form/form elements is written well and that the form on your site is easy to use at all screen sizes. In this tutorial, you will write CSS that covers `input [type=text,radio,checkbox]`, `select`, `submit`, `button`, `textarea`, and `label`.

First, create a form and add it to a page. The one I'm using, which includes all of the elements that need to be styled (except the input type "button," which will accept the same properties as the submit button), is shown in **Figure 7.7**.

Figure 7.7 The form, completely unstyled.

In this tutorial, we are going to start at the mobile level, adding basic styles and working up from there. The first step I recommend you take is to wrap your contact form in its own div, or use the `.page` or `.post` class to ensure that you don't

mess up forms elsewhere on the site (e.g., comment forms). Contact Form 7 will automatically use the class .wpcf7.

By default, Contact Form 7 will create a simple, readymade contact form using <p> tags as wrappers. While there is nothing technically wrong about doing this (the forms will display just fine), it's more semantically correct to use <div> because the content is not text, it's a form field. Here is the form as it looks in the WordPress admin after some modifications:

```
<div class="mf-contact-form">
    <div><label>Your Name (required)</label>[text* your-name]
    →</div>

    <div><label>Your Email (required)</label>[email* your-email]
    →</div>

    <div><label>Your Favorite Team</label> [radio radio-557
    →use_label_element "Yankees" "Red Sox" "Mets" "Phillies"]
    →</div>

    <div><label>Teams You'd See Play?</label>[checkbox
    →checkbox-887 use_label_element "Yankees" "Red Sox" "Mets"
    →"Phillies"]</div>

    <div><label>State</label>[select menu-255 include_blank
    →"New York" "Mass" "PA" "Alabama" "Alaska" "Arizona"]</div>

    <div><label>Your Message</label>[textarea your-message]
    →</div>

    <div>[submit "Send"]</div>
</div>
```

With that, here are some basic styles:

```
.wpcf7 form{
    text-align: left;
    font-size: 1.25em;
    max-width: 95%;
    }
```

```
.wpcf7 form{
    text-align: left;
    font-size: 1.25em;
    max-width: 95%;
    }

.wpcf7 form div{
    margin: 15px 0;
    text-align: left;
    }

.wpcf7 form div label{
    text-align: left;
    max-width: 98%;
    display: block;
    font-size: 1.4em;
    font-weight: bold;
    }

.wpcf7 form div input, .wpcf7 form div select, .wpcf7 form
→div textarea{
    padding: 5px;
    width: 95%;
    }

.wpcf7 form div input[type='checkbox'], .wpcf7 form
→div input[type='radio']{
    width: auto;
    }

.wpcf7 form div textarea{
    height: 150px;
    }

.wpcf7 form div input[type="submit"]{
    width: 100%;
    border-radius: 10px;
    -webkit-border-radius: 10px;
```

```
    -moz-border-radius: 10px;
    background: -webkit-linear-gradient(#b5b5b5 0%,
    →#eeeded 100%);
    border: 1px solid #999999;
    }

.wpcf7 form div input[type="submit"]:hover{
    border: 1px solid #CFCFCF;
    }
```

These basic styles turn the mess shown in Figure 7.7 into a reasonably good-looking form (**Figure 7.8**).

Figure 7.8 The new form, post-CSS.

Most of what is there is self-explanatory, but I want to touch on a few lines. I set a max-width for `.wpfc7 form` and the form elements, and a set width for the label element. Without these widths, the text boxes and text areas would fly off the screen in some cases, so we're using CSS to limit the width.

In the case of the labels, a set width coupled with the line `display: block` ensures that the label gets its own line, and in the case of the checkboxes and radio buttons, each element gets its own line. With Contact Form 7, you can choose to wrap the entire form element in a label, which is what I opted to do. The resulting markup is something like this (I have removed some of the extra markup the plugin adds):

```
<label><input type="checkbox" name="watch-teams[]"
 →value="Yankees">  Yankees</label>
```

Finally, I made the labels a bit larger and added extra padding to the textboxes so they are easier for users to select using just their thumb when using a mobile device.

Expanding outward, the form doesn't actually look bad, but the space can be better used; you'll fix that at the next breakpoint. Where the breakpoint occurs is largely up to you. You should decide where the form starts to look bad/lopsided and how it conforms to your template. That's how I picked mine!

Our goal, once the breakpoint is decided, is to make better use of the space. With a wider screen, there doesn't need to be as much vertical content. In the following CSS, better use of space will be achieved in three ways: decrease the font size, compact the form, and line up the radio buttons and checkboxes side by side. Let's get to it:

```
@media screen and (min-width: 40.688em){
    .wpcf7 form{
        margin: 10px auto;
        width: 80%;
        }
    .wpcf7 form div{
        padding: 10px 0;
        clear: left;
        }
    .wpcf7 form .wpcf7-list-item{
        width: 48%;
        float: left;
        margin: 10px 0;
        }
```

```
.wpcf7 form div label{
    font-size: 1em;
    font-weight: normal;
    }
.wpcf7 form div input, .wpcf7 form div select, .wpcf7 form
→div textarea{
    width: 55%;
    margin-left: 2%;
}

.wpcf7 form div input[type='checkbox'], .wpcf7 form
→div input[type='radio']{
    width: auto;
    }

.wpcf7 form div input[type="submit"]{
    width: 50%;
    margin: 0 2%;
    }
}
```

Several things are going on here. First, the max-width of the form is 80%. This is in place so as users expand out, the form won't look too wide or spaced out. There are also several styles to "neutralize" the mobile styles. The form labels are no longer bold and have returned to the normal font size of 1em. Form fields have a max-width of around 50% to prevent them from getting too long for users. The divs get spaced out a bit, and, finally, the checkboxes and radio buttons are changed to two per line.

Here, I had to rely on one of Contact Form 7's generated classes, `.wpcf7-list-item`. This is a class that gets wrapped around both the form element and the label, allowing me to set a width and float it. As you can imagine, as you expand even wider, you can adjust the widths accordingly. You will see that in the next tutorial.

You can see the final product in **Figure 7.9**.

Figure 7.9 The form in a full-width, wide-screen device.

How to Build a Responsive WordPress Products Page

Presenting products in an easy way for website visitors to view is an incredibly important task for anyone running an online catalog or e-commerce site. On Black Friday 2012, 24% of online traffic came from mobile devices! Luckily, we can do that with a CPT and CSS.

This will only be the catalog page, since single-post pages have been covered extensively throughout the book. The goal here is to see how a responsive grid works.

NOTE

This will not be an e-commerce site, just a site that displays products in an easy way for consumers to browse. If you use something like WP e-Commerce (http://rwdwp. com/92), you should be able to translate the CSS pretty easily.

First, let's start with the CPT. As in the other tutorials, you should create a folder and file of the same name within the /plugins/ directory. I'll call mine /mf-catalog/ and mf-catalog.php. Here's the top of mf-catalog.php:

```
/*
Plugin Name: Millennium Flights Products Page
Plugin URI: http://millenniumflights.com
Description: A simple plugin that creates and display products
    →with WordPress using custom post types!
Author: Joe Casabona
Version: 1.0
Author URI: http://www.casabona.org
*/

/*Some Set-up*/
define('MFP_PATH', WP_PLUGIN_URL . '/' . plugin_basename(
    →dirname(__FILE__) ) . '/' );
define('MFP_NAME', "Millenium Flights Products");

/*Files to Include*/
require_once('mf-products-cpt.php');
```

You'll see the same approach taken in other plugins, with the plugin definition followed by some constants for later reference.

The Shortcode and Template Tag

When the CPT is built out, there will be a set list of fields you can use to display the content. Since it's only a catalog and not a full e-commerce plugin, you can cut out a lot of fields that don't necessarily apply. Here's the info → field mapping:

◆ Name of Product → Title

◆ Description of Product → Editor

◆ Price → Text Box

◆ Main Image → Featured Image

◆ Category → Taxonomy

The first thing you should do is create a single function that both the shortcode and template tag can call:

```
function mfp_get_products(){
    $products= '<div class="mf-catalog">';

    $args= "post_type=products";
    $catalog= new WP_Query($args);


     while($catalog->have_posts()) : $catalog->the_post();
        $img= mfp_get_image();
        $price= mfp_get_the_price($post->ID);
        $products.='<div class="mf-product">'.$img.'
                <p><strong>'. get_the_title() .'</strong>:
                →'. get_the_excerpt() .'</p>
                <p class="price">'. $price .'</p>
        </div>';

    endwhile;

    wp_reset_postdata();


    $products.= '</div>';

    return $products;
}
```

The approach is the same as the one you took with the slider plugin. Use `WP_Query` to grab each product from the CPT that you'll create later, and simply print the information on screen. Unlike the slider, however, instead of using `get_the_post_thumbnail()` to get the featured image, you'll create a function later called `mfp_get_image()`. This will return an `<img>` element and allow you to use a properly sized image if you choose to use it elsewhere. The shortcode and template tag will just call the main function:

```php
/**The Shortcode**/
function mfp_shortcode($atts, $content=null){

    $products= mfp_get_products();

    return $products;

}

add_shortcode('mf_products', 'mfp_shortcode');

/**The Template Tag**/
function mfp_products_tag(){

    print mfp_get_slider();
}
```

Building the Custom Post Type

The CPT for this plugin will be a little more complicated than the slider one. In mf-products-cpt.php, add the following code:

```php
define('MFP_CPT_NAME', "Products");
define('MFP_CPT_SINGLE', "Product");
define('MFP_CPT_TYPE', "products");
add_theme_support('post-thumbnails', array('products'));

function mfp_register() {
    $args = array(
        'label' => __(MFP_CPT_NAME),
        'singular_label' => __(MFP_CPT_SINGLE),
        'public' => true,
        'show_ui' => true,
        'capability_type' => 'post',
        'hierarchical' => false,
        'rewrite' => true,
        'supports' => array('title', 'editor', 'thumbnail')
    );
```

```
    register_post_type(MFP_CPT_TYPE , $args );
  register_taxonomy("product-category", array("products"),
  →array("hierarchical" => true, "label" => "Product Categories",
  →"singular_label" => "Product Category", "rewrite" => true));


}


add_action('init', 'mfp_register');
```

You'll see here, unlike the slider, this CPT is accepting one extra field for the price and a custom taxonomy for the product's category. The taxonomy is located in the same function where you register the post:

```
register_taxonomy("product-category", array("products"),
→array("hierarchical" => true, "label" => "Product Categories",
→"singular_label" => "Product Category", "rewrite" => true));
```

This function (which has been part of WordPress since version 2.8) sends the following information, which will be used to automatically add a "Category" box to the CPT:

◆ The name of the new taxonomy

◆ An array of Post Types it should be applied to

◆ An array that specifies the following:

◆ Whether there can be parent/child categories

◆ The menu label for both the plural and singular

◆ Whether WordPress should create mod_rewrite rules (for pretty permalinks) for this CPT

◆ What the category slug should be

There are also many more arguments, which you can read about in the Codex (http://rwdwp.com/93). When you're creating a new taxonomy for a CPT, I strongly recommend that you place `register_taxonomy()` directly after `register_post_type()`. If you don't, you may see this error:

```
Fatal error: Call to a member function add_rewrite_tag()
→on a non-object...
```

Once that's taken care of, it's time to add the new field, for price, in:

```php
add_action("admin_init", "mfp_meta_box");

function mfp_meta_box(){
    add_meta_box("mf-products", "Product Price",
      →"mfp_meta_options", "products", "side", "low");
}

function mfp_meta_options(){
        global $post;
        if ( defined('DOING_AUTOSAVE') && DOING_AUTOSAVE )
          →return $post_id;
        $custom = get_post_custom($post->ID);
        $mfpPrice = $custom["mpf-price"][0];
?>
    <label>Price:</label><input name="mfp-price" value="<?php
      →echo $mfpPrice; ?>" />
<?php
        }
```

We use add_action() to call the function mfp_meta_box() when the WordPress admin is created. Our function will add another box to the CPT, which will be populated with the function named as the third argument, mfp_meta_options().

In mfp_meta_options(), a form is created that will allow users to add a price from the add post page. The first thing the function does is grab the $post array, which will give you access to the custom fields for the post being edited. In the next line, the function is checking to make sure WordPress isn't currently saving the post or custom fields; if it is, the information will not be saved and things will break because the information being added will be overwritten with blank strings.

If WordPress is not doing a save, we grab the custom fields for the current post and create a form field using that info. Then we get any preexisting values so that the user doesn't have to enter them every time he or she wants to edit a given post. The function get_post_custom() accepts a post ID as an argument and will return a 2D associative array containing all of the post's custom data. In this case, there is only one entry, $mfpPrice. Since technically there can be multiple values for each CPT—that is, each post could possibly have multiple prices because of the way WordPress stores meta fields—this information is always returned as an

Want to make a Portfolio CPT?

As it turns out, the Products CPT can be easily converted to a Portfolio CPT just by changing a few fields. First, you'll want to change all instances of "product(s)" to "project(s)."

After that, convert the "price" custom field to "project link." Finally, in your presentation function, replace the function that returns price with a function that returns a working link. Assuming you call your project link field mfProjectLink:

```
function mf_project_link($pid, $newWindow=true){
    $site= get_post_custom_values('mfProjectLink', $pid);
    $target= ($newWindow) ? 'target="_blank"' : '';
    return ($site[0] != "") ? '<a class="mf-project-link" '.
    →$target .' href="'.$site[0].'">Visit the Site</a>' :
    →'<em class="mfp-no-link">Live Link Unavailable</em>';
}
```

The function accepts two arguments: the first is the post ID, and the second is whether we want the link to open in a new window, which defaults to true.

array. To grab the first value (and in this case the only value), we need to specify index 0. Then, the function will print the form field using the data (if any) returned.

Next, it's time to add a Save function for when the custom data is submitted:

```
add_action('save_post', 'mfp_save_custom_data');

function mfp_save_custom_data(){
    global $post;

    if ( defined('DOING_AUTOSAVE') && DOING_AUTOSAVE ){
        return $post_id;
    }else{
        update_post_meta($post->ID, "mfpPrice",
        →$_POST["mfpPrice"]);
    }
}
```

The hook this time calls the function when the post is saved. It again grabs the $post array so we can get the post ID and check to see if the post is autosaving. If you don't include this line, you'll lose the data, so it's important to keep that in.

If the post is not updating, save the custom fields using update_post_meta(), sending the post ID, the name of the custom field, and the new value. It's also worth noting that update_post_meta will escape the string for you before inserting it into the database, so security issues like SQL injections should not be an issue.

ADDING THE FUNCTIONS TO RETURN VALUES

There is still one thing that needs to be taken care of: the two functions we call in mfp_get_products(). One is a simple one to return the price:

```
function mfp_get_the_price($pid){
    $custom = get_post_custom($pid);
        return $custom["mpf-price"][0];
}
```

It might only be a two-liner, but it will make things a bit easier to manage down the road. Then there is the image function:

```
function mfp_get_images($pid=NULL, $size='thumbnail'){
    $url= wp_get_attachment_image_src( get_post_thumbnail_
    →id($pid), $size);
    return '<img src="'.$url[0] .'" alt="'. esc_attr(get_the_
    →title($pid)) .'" />';
}
```

This is also a fairly simple function that accepts a post ID (default to NULL), which will use the current post, and a size (default to thumbnail) and returns an image element with a URL and the post's title as the alternate text. In this plugin, the thumbnail is used as the default since it's a small square image that will work well on any device. If you want to create a differently sized square image, you can do this by adding your own image size.

With the programming done, it's time to focus on this display. The goal here is to provide basic CSS to style the products without being intrusive on the themes. It's likely that plugin users will provide their own CSS.

The first thing to do is add a function to include a style sheet in the theme:

```
function mfp_scripts() {
    wp_enqueue_style('mfp-css', MFP_PATH.'/mfp-style.css');
}

add_action( 'wp_enqueue_scripts', 'mfp_scripts' );
```

This function can be used for any style sheets or JavaScript you might want to add to this function. In the mfp-style.css file, there will be some groundwork for a responsive products page, starting with the smaller screens:

```
.mf-catalog img{
    max-width: 100%;
    height: auto;
    }

.mf-product{
    text-align: center;
    margin: 10px 2%;
    border: 1px solid #999999;
    background: #FFFFFF;
    padding: 5px 2%;
    }

.mf-product p{
    text-align: left;
    }

.mf-product p.price{
    font-weight: bold;
    color: #880000;
    }
```

Most of the CSS will be here. It's setting the products apart from other content with basic backgrounds and borders, and it's ensuring that the images resize properly.

Moving on from here, the toughest part is resizing when the thumbnails start to look too small. Here I will assume that there are no sidebars on the page, resizing three times for two, three, and four columns:

```
@media screen and (min-width: 37.938em){

    .mf-product{
        max-width: 40%;
        }
}

@media screen and (min-width: 67.1013em){

    .mf-product{
        max-width: 25%;
        }
}

@media screen and (min-width: 67.1013em){

    .mf-product{
        max-width: 25%;
        }
}

@media screen and (min-width: 106.563em){

    .mf-product{
        max-width: 15%;
        }
}
```

Notice that the only thing that's changing is the max-width of the mf-product div. The styles set earlier should take care of the rest. Here's what the final product looks like, both on mobile and as four columns (**Figure 7.10**).

Figure 7.10   The catalog on mobile and as a four-column page.

Wrapping Up

Throughout the chapter we looked at a lot of different tutorials for adding features and functionality to WordPress. You may have noticed some repetition in some places, especially with CSS or Custom Post Types. It's important to remember the techniques that were discussed throughout the book in order to make a truly responsive theme or plugin. Remember: RWD is not just about making a website fit on small screens.

In the interest of time and space, these were also relatively basic tutorials. The goal was not necessarily to make a production-ready, never-before-seen plugin. The goal was to look at a good way to do these things responsively. Now it's time to take these techniques and apply them to the really cool things that we are working on!

Questions

1. The default gallery markup isn't really a great way to make responsive galleries. How do you change the gallery's default markup?

2. When is it OK to use the PHP `extract()` function?

3. What's the trade-off between using a plugin's CSS sheet and embedding the CSS into your own style.css?

4. Why is it important to use `wp_enqueue_script()`?

Answers

1. Replace the function the `[gallery]` shortcode calls with your own, using this code:

   ```
   remove_shortcode('gallery', 'gallery_shortcode');
   add_shortcode('gallery', 'my_gallery_shortcode');
   ```

2. Only within functions where you know the scope of all the variables, as to not accidentally overwrite variables and cause unexpected results.

3. Copying the CSS into your own style.css ensures your theme is making one less HTTP request, but it ties your plugin to your theme.

4. By using `wp_enqueue_script()`, you are ensuring that multiple copies of the same script are not being loaded, which lightens the page as well as reduces the risk of conflicts.

Appendix

Resources

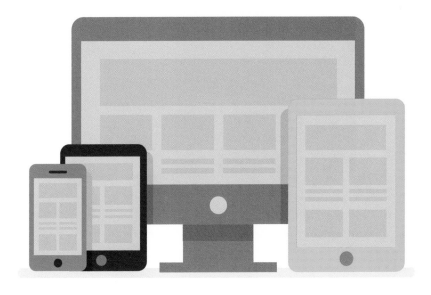

A Few Words to Sum Up

In the eternal words of a certain cartoon pig, "That's all, folks!" I went into writing this book knowing how great both WordPress and Responsive Web Design are, and knowing that they could come together to help us make great websites. But I also learned a lot along the way, as it goes when you write a book.

I hope you take what you learned here and do truly great things. I hope you improve upon what I've coded; after all, the web is a living, breathing thing that is constantly changing. That's why we have Responsive Web Design in the first place, right? Remember that moving forward, we will almost certainly have a host of new devices to deliver our content to. Explorers are testing Google Glass, the first smart watches are coming to market, and who knows what else tech companies are working on. Perhaps soon a website will be projected right into the palms of our hands.

I also want to thank you for reading. I hope you got as much enjoyment out of reading this book as I did writing it. And if you're champing at the bit for more, there are a lot of great resources out there for both WordPress and Responsive Web Design, from websites to books to meetups. In the remaining pages, I've listed some of the best out there.

NOTE
All of the links mentioned throughout the book are available at the book's website, http://rwdwp.com/links/.

Responsive Design with WordPress

Pre-Order   Pre-Order on Amazon

Responsive Design with WordPress shows readers Responsive Web Design principles, as well as how to develop responsively when using WordPress. With a greater push towards mobile and the emergence of Responsive Web Design (RWD), more and more WordPress developers are looking to create responsive themes for their websites. The book goes into detail, covering what default CSS

About the Author: Joe Casabona is a web developer, teacher, speaker, and writer currently working for the University of Scranton. He has been making websites since 2002, and using WordPress since 2004. He previously wrote Building WordPress Themes from Scratch for Rockable

Books

Building WordPress Themes from Scratch

Joe Casabona, Rockable Press, 2012.

My first book will take you through the process of creating a WordPress theme out of HTML and CSS files. I teach you how to use WordPress, as well as how to leverage the API to create your own custom themes, plugins, and content types. We'll also look at how to create widgets, theme options, and more.

Web Designer's Guide to WordPress: Plan, Theme, Build, Launch

Jesse Friedman, New Riders, 2012.

If you want to dig deeper into WordPress, Jesse Friedman's book will take you through the entire WordPress process, from installing and using it, to developing themes, plugins, and shortcodes, to testing and launching. I highly recommend it!

Professional WordPress: Design and Development

Brad Williams, David Damstra, Hal Stern, WROX, 2013.

This comprehensive work focuses squarely on development, looking at plugin and theme development, security, scaling, spam, and more. This team does great work, and this is a book that should be on every WordPress developer's bookshelf.

WordPress for Web Developers

Stephanie Leary, Apress, 2013

Stephanie's fantastic resource takes you from installing WordPress and using every facet of the admin panel to deploying it securely on your server, to developing themes. It really is a one-stop shop for WordPress use/development.

Responsive Web Design

Ethan Marcotte, A Book Apart, 2011

The first book written on the topic, this provides an incredible base and teaches you everything you need to know to get started in RWD. It has examples, code, and some best practices to help you create great responsive sites.

Mobile First

Luke Wroblewski, A Book Apart, 2011

This book goes hand in hand with *Responsive Web Design*. There is no hands-on coding, but there are stats, screens, and lots of great reasons why when you design a website, you should take a "Mobile First" approach and start from the smallest screen.

Implementing Responsive Design

Tim Kadlec, New Riders, 2012.

After reading *Responsive Web Design*, this should be your next stop. Tim Kadlec builds upon everything from Ethan Marcotte's book while talking about more recent developments in the field regarding better practices, as well as RESS, workflow, and more.

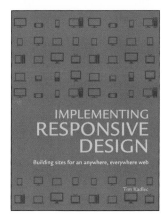

Meetups

Meetups are a great way to network with individuals, talk through problems, and learn!

Meetup.com

http://www.meetup.com/

Meetup.com is the definitive place to find meetups in your area. I recommend doing searches for "WordPress," "Web Design," and "Tech." The site will also ask you for some words to describe you if you create an account, and then it will recommend meetups near you.

WordCamp Central

http://central.wordcamp.org/

WordCamps are conferences that focus solely on WordPress, and they are fantastic. They are held all over the world and attract all kinds of WordPress users from bloggers to developers. WordCamp Central features a list of upcoming events as well as links to talks from previous camps.

An Event Apart

http://aneventapart.com/

An Event Apart conferences bring in the best in the business, including some of the authors listed above. These are two-day, single-track conferences with an optional workshop on the third day, and they are packed with tons of information regarding the latest and greatest in the field. They are held in various cities throughout the United States.

Links

Though all of the links mentioned in the book are located at http://rwdwp.com/links/, there are some great online resources that were not mentioned in the book. Here's a quick list:

Websites

1. A List Apart: http://alistapart.com
2. Brad Frost: http://bradfrostweb.com
3. *net Magazine:* http://creativebloq.com/net-magazine
4. *Smashing Magazine:* www.smashingmagazine.com
5. Tuts+: https://tutsplus.com/
6. Luke Wroblewski: http://lukew.com
7. This Is Responsive: http://responsive.rga.com/
8. CSS-Tricks: http://css-tricks.com/

Podcasts

1. The Big Web Show: www.muleradio.net/thebigwebshow/
2. Happy Monday Podcast: http://happymondaypodcast.com/
3. Shop Talk Show: http://shoptalkshow.com/
4. The Gently Mad: http://thegentlymad.com/

Index